The Little Big Book of Wisdom

Dean Kalahar

For my students: past, present, & future

With deepest respect and gratitude to my intellectual mentor, Dr. Thomas Sowell

The following is a compilation of knowledge gathered over the last 30 years of teaching, mentoring, and counseling students as a public school educator. The words contain powerful life lessons and cognitive realizations that are necessary for any student who wants to rise above intellectual mediocrity, or just needs guidance in paddling through the white water of life.

These intellectual gems can be a valuable tool for personal growth, and have served as a buoy to many students who were not afraid to change the recipe in life's cookbook. The hope is that in sharing them with you, additional benefits will be realized.

This work also puts together some of the most important thoughts from the influential leaders who defined our national history and culture. Herein one will find humble words every American should be familiar with. They offer our culture a defense against forgetting who we are by remembering who we were so we may continue to move forward.

Many of the ideas might, as my students would say, "rock your world" or "blow your mind" with dissonant cognitions that can't be ignored. Let them be a source for honing your mental machete so you can offer inspiration or perspiration depending on your challenge.

The depth of these thoughts is significant, the dexterity of words is inspiring, and the wisdom is worth pondering.

Enjoy,

Dean

Table of Topics: **Page**

Abortion

Abortion is almost always wrapped in the velvety euphemisms of "women's health" and "reproductive choice." It should tell you something when passionate advocates of unrestricted abortion are so uncomfortable talking about ... abortion. - Jonah Goldberg

Addiction

Criminality is a better predictor of addiction then addiction is of criminality. -Anthony Daniels

Affirmative action

Ninety-two percent of blacks at elite colleges are from the top half of the income distribution. A study a decade ago at Harvard Law School found that only a third of black students had four African-American grandparents. Another third were from interracial families, and the rest were children of recent immigrants from Africa or the West Indies. –Mona Charon

Affordability

If everything were made more affordable, there would still not be any more to go around when things were prohibitively expensive. –Thomas Sowell

Anti-trust laws

Anti-trust laws promote the idea, "those who can, compete, those who can't, lobby. -Arnold Kling

Bigotry

The essence of bigotry is denying others the same rights you claim for yourself. -Thomas Sowell

Black Family

In 1950, female-headed households were 18 percent of the black population. Today it's close to 70 percent. One study of 19th-century slave families found that in up to three-fourths of the families, all the children lived with the biological mother and father. In 1925 New York City, 85 percent of black households were two-parent households. Herbert Gutman, author of "The Black Family in Slavery and Freedom, 1750-1925," reports, "Five in six children under the age of six lived with both parents." Also, both during slavery and as late as 1920, a teenage girl raising a child without a man present was rare among blacks.

A study of 1880 family structure in Philadelphia found that three-quarters of black families were nuclear families (composed of two parents and children). What is significant, given today's arguments that slavery and discrimination decimated the black family structure, is the fact that years ago, there were only slight differences in family structure among racial groups.

Coupled with the dramatic breakdown in the black family structure has been an astonishing growth in the rate of illegitimacy. The black illegitimacy rate in 1940 was about 14 percent; black illegitimacy today is over 70 percent, and in some cities, it is over 80 percent...

The Census Bureau pegs the poverty rate among blacks at 28.1 percent. A statistic that one never hears about is that the poverty rate among intact married black families has been in the single digits for more than two decades, currently at 8.4 percent. Weak family structures not only spell poverty and dependency but also contribute to the social pathology seen in many black communities -- for example, violence and predatory sex. Each year, roughly 7,000 blacks are murdered. Ninety-four percent of the time, the murderer is another black person. Though blacks are 13 percent of the nation's population, they account for more than 50 percent of homicide victims. Nationally, the black homicide victimization rate is six times that of whites, and in some cities, it's 22 times that of whites. According to the Bureau of Justice Statistics, between 1976 and 2011, there were 279,384 black murder victims. Coupled with being most of the nation's homicide victims, blacks are also major victims of violent personal crimes, such as assault, rape and robbery.

To put this violence in perspective, black fatalities during the Korean War (3,075), Vietnam War (7,243) and all wars since 1980 (about 8,200) come to about 18,500, a number that pales in comparison

with black loss of life at home. Young black males had a greater chance of reaching maturity on the battlefields of Iraq and Afghanistan than on the streets of Philadelphia, Chicago, Detroit, Oakland, Newark and other cities.
-Blacks must confront reality; Walter Williams, August 27, 2014.

Capitalism

Capitalism is the astounding belief that the most wickedest of men will do the most wickedest of things for the greatest good of everyone.
-John Maynard Keynes

Capitalism works better than it sounds, while socialism sounds better than it works. -Richard Nixon

Despite the name, capitalism is not an "ism." It is not a philosophy but an economy. -Thomas Sowell

The problem with social organization is how to set up an arrangement under which greed will do the least harm; capitalism is that kind of a system. -Milton Friedman

All people, however fanatical they may be in their zeal to disparage and to fight capitalism, implicitly pay homage to it by passionately clamoring for the products it turns out. -Ludwig Von Mises

Capitalism teaches people to work harder; the welfare state teaches people to want harder. -Dennis Prager

The inherent vice of capitalism is the unequal sharing of blessings; the inherent virtue of socialism is the equal sharing of miseries.
-Winston Churchill

We are fond of saying that the answer to free-speech problems is more free speech. But we seem incapable of grasping that sometimes — and only sometimes — the solution to capitalism's problems is more capitalism. –Jonah Goldberg

In the contemporary world, where left-wing attitudes are regarded as normative, it is a given that capitalism, with its free market and profit

motive, emanates from and creates selfishness, while socialism, the welfare state, and the "social compact" as it is increasingly referred to, emanate from and produce selflessness. The opposite is the truth.
-Dennis Prager

The capitalist achievement does not typically consist in providing more silk stockings for queens but in bringing them within the reach of factory girls in return for steadily decreasing amounts of effort...The capitalist process, not by coincidence but by virtue of its mechanism, progressively raises the standard of life of the masses through a perennial gale of creative destruction.- Joseph Schumpeter

Those critical of America are not the purported victims of its supposedly rapacious capitalist system, but more often those in the arts, universities, media, and government, who have the time and leisure to contemplate utopian perfection without firsthand and daily exposure to backbreaking physical labor, relentless bullies, or unapologetically violent criminals.
-Victor Davis Hansen

Many times, if not always, the market will offer choices that are less than ideal. Acceptance of this reality and working within a framework that applies economic evidence and logic will afford the economy with the best possible decision making processes and policy decisions. Expecting perfection by pointing out the less than perfect case scenario the market provides, in order to win political points, sound compassionate, or offer humanistic demagoguery, will create inefficiencies, retard economic growth and lower the standard of living. Understandably, the market does not always seem like the fairest or most compassionate way to deal with the realities of what, how, and for whom. But those who can see beyond the dogma of the self anointed purveyors of conventional wisdom and the suffering their command approach creates will promote an intelligent market economy that looks to no one for its success yet forgets no one in its rewards. -Dean Kalahar

What is called "capitalism" might more accurately be called consumerism. It is the consumers who call the tune, and those capitalists who want to remain capitalists have to learn to dance to it.
-Thomas Sowell

Anyone who saw East Berlin and West Berlin during the years when communism prevailed in the eastern part of the city and a market economy in the rest of it could not help noticing the sharp contrast between the prosperity of West Berlin and the poverty in East Berlin. -Thomas Sowell

In 1607, 105 men and boys, mostly indentured servants who held no private property and were to work for the "common store," disembarked from three ships and established the first permanent settlement in America…By 1609, there were 500 settlers, including women. And yet within six months fewer than 100 were still alive during what came to be known as "the starving time." Why? According to a governor of the colony, George Percy, most of the colonists died of famine, despite the "good and fruitful" soil, the abundant deer and turkey, and the "strawberries, raspberries and fruits unknown" growing wild. And yet people were desperate. They ate dogs and cats, then rats and mice. They apparently ate their deceased neighbors. And some said that one man murdered and ate his pregnant wife. By the spring, they had given up. They abandoned the fort and boarded ships to return to England. But, miraculously, as they sailed out of Chesapeake Bay, they encountered three ships with new recruits, so they turned around and tried to make another go of it. The additional settlers and supplies kept them alive. When a new governor, Thomas Dale, arrived a year after the starving time, he was shocked to find the settlers bowling in the streets instead of working. Dale's most important reform was to institute private property. He understood that *men who don't benefit from their hard work tend not to work very hard*. As such he allotted every man three acres of land and freed them to work for themselves. And then, the Virginia historian Matthew Page Andrews wrote, "As soon as the settlers were thrown upon their own resources, and each freeman had acquired the right of owning property, the colonists quickly developed what became the distinguishing characteristic of Americans—an aptitude for all kinds of craftsmanship coupled with an innate genius for experimentation and invention." The Jamestown colony became a success, people from all over Europe flocked to the New World, and capitalism was born in America.-David Boaz

Prior to the rise of capitalism, the way people amassed great wealth was by fraud, theft, dishonesty, lobbying, looting, plundering, and enslaving their fellow man. Capitalism made it possible to become wealthy by serving one's fellow man. –Walter Williams

One thing we have learned from hundreds of experiments in shared, communal living, from the pilgrim settlers or the hippie communes or the artists' colonies or the kibbutzes, up to the size of communist China, is that they almost always fail. We are simply not spiritually advanced enough, as a whole, to operate in that fashion. We never have been, and probably never will be…Smith saw that this rampant self-interest was channeled by the capitalist system – basically a system of private property and common law – into activity that would benefit others. Those focused on wealth and power, instead of using rape, plunder, pillage and enslavement, as was common through millennia of history, would have to provide some sort of useful good or service to others, in a way that provided a profit. Those chasing wealth and power would find that the easiest path to their goal would be to provide something beneficial for society as a whole. –Nathan Lewis

"Capitalism" has elements that go by the code words "free market" or "laissez-faire." These are labels for rather complex, sophisticated ideas that would take tens of thousands of words to explain in full. They don't mean that "anything goes" or "do what thou wilst." Capitalism is a system of rules, finely tuned to produce certain beneficial outcomes, even if the participants themselves have no interest in the condition of society as a whole. The virtue is in the system. –Nathan Lewis

It would be all too easy for us, among the wealthiest people who have ever lived, in one of the richest places on earth, to disdain the institutions that have enabled us to escape the strictures of poverty and disrespect that have plagued humanity for the vast majority of its existence. Our crime today, however, would lie not in our inequalities but rather in our refusal to uphold the institutions that give humanity the only hope it has ever known of rising out of its natural state of destitution. The great and precious blessings of freedom and prosperity that we Americans have enjoyed, and that some, but not enough, others around the world have also experienced, deserve nothing less. -James Otteson

Capitalism is part of a larger set of social institutions that has another justification for itself than increasing material prosperity, as important as that is. And that is its presumption of the dignity and preciousness of each individual and the respect that that demands. Capitalism assumes that each of us is a free moral agent, capable of leading his own life, of holding his head up, not begging leave or permission before he acts, not subject to correction from his superiors: a citizen, not a subject. Capitalism does not suppose that we are infallible; on the contrary, it is because no one is infallible that capitalism denies any of us absolute authority over others' lives. It assumes only that as free moral agents, each of us has authority over himself and that each of us is sovereign over his own life. -James Otteson

Capitalism's success at its stated goals has been so enormous and unprecedented that we might easily think that that is all that can be said on its behalf. Rescuing hundreds of millions of people from grinding poverty is, however, nothing to sneeze at—and nothing to take for granted. The rest of human history has shown us just how nasty, poor, and brutish the default for human life is; even the twentieth century—that age of democratic enlightenment—has vividly demonstrated how quickly civilization can turn to barbarism. Peace, the rule of law, and steadily rising standards of living are the exception, not the rule, and the institutions that uphold them are fragile and require constant maintenance and nurturing. -James Otteson

Since 1800, the world's population has increased sixfold; yet despite this enormous increase, real income per person has increased approximately 16-fold. That is a truly amazing achievement. In America, the increase is even more dramatic: in 1800, the total population in America was 5.3 million, life expectancy was 39, and the real gross domestic product per capita was $1,343 (in 2010 dollars); in 2011, our population was 308 million, our life expectancy was 78, and our GDP per capita was $48,800. Thus even while the population increased 58-fold, our life expectancy doubled, and our GDP per capita increased almost 36-fold. Such growth is unprecedented in the history of humankind. Considering that worldwide per-capita real income for the previous 99.9 percent of human existence averaged consistently around $1 per day, that is extraordinary. –James Otteson

It takes a subtle and sophisticated understanding of paradoxical truths to comprehend a competitive free enterprise market entrepreneurial capital exchange economy. –Dean Kalahar

"The accumulation of capital" is a fancy phrase for "the conservation of resources." To accumulate capital, you've got to spend less than your income, which leaves more goods available for the rest of us. How could anyone object to that? If you nevertheless believe that the capitalists have been busily rigging the system in their own interest, you've got to admit they've done a spectacularly bad job of it. How else to explain the quintuple taxation of capital income, where you can invest a dollar that was taxed the day you earned it, then pay corporate income taxes, dividend taxes, capital gains taxes and inheritance taxes on the income it throws off? Surely any concern that the rich are calling the policy shots should melt away in the face of actual policy. In fact, there are good reasons in theory to suppose that things work the other way — in a democracy, it's much easier for the 99% to exploit the 1% than the other way around, and the richer the 1% get, the more vulnerable they become. -Steve Landsberg

Central planning

Although painted with the best of intentions, the inefficient actions of central planning does not make the reality any less harmful. In the end, central planning leads to a total breakdown of civility and sharing, the abuse of position, and the collective suffering of the masses due to elites commanding inefficiency and tyranny. -Dean Kalahar

Even if a small group believed they could command and create the perfect society, a utopia without freedom is just a fancy name for a prison. -Dean Kalahar

Unfortunately, the relation between the ends and the mean remains widely misunderstood. Many of those who profess the most individualistic objectives support collectivist means without recognizing the contradiction. It is tempting to believe that social evils arise from the activities of evil men and that if only good men (like ourselves, naturally) wielded power, all would be well. That view requires only emotion and self praise-easy to come by and satisfying as well. To understand why it is the 'good' men in positions of power will produce evil, while the ordinary man without power but able to engage in voluntary cooperation with his neighbors will produce good, requires analysis and thought, subordinating the emotions to the rational faculty. Surely that is one answer to the perennial mystery of why collectivism,

14

with its demonstrated record of producing tyranny and misery, is so widely regarded as superior to individualism, with its demonstrated record of producing freedom and plenty. -Milton Friedman

Milton Friedman once challenged anyone to name just one place on the globe that has had anything other than a totalitarian/dictatorial command economy for the majority of its existence. With few exceptions—notably the United States during the latter part of the 18th century through the early part of the 20th century, early Greece, and Italy during the Renaissance—man has not provided himself with the most beneficial economic systems or behaviors. -Dean Kalahar

When the government creates some new program, nothing is easier than to show whatever the benefits that program produces. Indeed, those who run the program will be more than cooperative in bringing those benefits to the attention of the media. But it is virtually impossible to trace the taxes that paid for the program back to their source and to show the alternative uses of that same money that could have been far more beneficial. -Thomas Sowell

Alternatives to a market economy may express nobler sentiments but the bottom line is whether this in fact leads to better behavior in terms of serving their fellow human being. -Thomas Sowell

The more the plans fail, the more the planners plan. -Ronald Reagan

Character

Choose silence of all virtues, for by it you hear other men's imperfections and conceal your own. -George Bernard Shaw

Willful shabbiness in circumstances demanding decorum is simply self important. -Kathleen Parker

It is not necessarily wise to start practicing austerities at the moment of crisis. -Kevin D. Williamson

Do not let success take you where character can't sustain you.
-Unknown via Dave Chappelle

It's not a sin to get knocked down; it's a sin not to get up.
–Carl M. Brashear

Nothing in the world can take the place of persistence. Talent will not; nothing is more common than unsuccessful men with talent. Genius will not; unrewarded genius is almost a proverb. Education will not; the world is full of educated derelicts. Persistence and determination are omnipotent. The slogan 'press on' has solved and always will solve the problems of the human race. -Calvin Coolidge

The shortest and surest way to live with honor in the world is to be in reality what we appear to be. -Socrates

Doing nothing in fear of making a mistake, is the greatest mistake you'll make. - Anonymous

If you're going through hell, keep going! -Winston Churchill

When assertive turns to attitude it becomes counterproductive. -Dean Kalahar

The way you dress on the outside shows what's on the inside. -Cassie Carpenter

If a man is not able to stand for something, he is liable to fall for anything. -Unknown

Knocked down seven times, get up eight. -Winston Churchill

There is a difference between can I and should I. -Dean Kalahar

Don't let your mouth write a check that your body can't cash. -Quincy Jones

Send not to know for whom the bell tolls, it tolls for thee. -John Donne

There is never the right time to do the wrong thing, but there is always a wrong time to do the right thing. –Lou Holtz

Well done is better than well said. -Benjamin Franklin

It's not the size of the dog in the fight, it's the size of the fight in the dog. -Mark Twain

A pessimist sees the difficulty in every opportunity; an optimist sees the opportunity in every difficulty. - Sir Winston Churchill

Successful people do all the things unsuccessful people don't want to do. –Unknown

If I know nothing yet have self respect, I will be wise. –Dean Kalahar

Self-confidence is quiet. –Dean Kalahar

Blaming others for one's own failures prolongs failure. -Richard Landes

I would rather be beaten in Right than succeed in Wrong. -James Garfield

History is full of examples of small groups who, believing in their cause, were resolved to stand by their guns. The only explanation for the meekness we observe is that the bourgeois order no longer makes any sense to the bourgeoisie itself and that, when all is said and nothing is done, it does not really care. -Joseph Schumpeter

All that glitters is not gold…gold in its native state is but dull, unornamental stuff, and that only low-born metals excite the admiration of the ignorant with an ostentatious glitter. However, like the rest of the world, I still go on underrating men of gold and glorifying men of mica. – Mark Twain

An arrow can only be shot by pulling it backward. When life is dragging you back with difficulties it means it's going to launch you into something great. So just focus and keep aiming. -Via Madison Garriott

At one time cultural norms use to act as a filter for choices and behavior, today the filter has been removed. The stench of the self-absorbed is no longer an affront because society has gotten use to the smell of cultural rot… What we have is an epidemic of distasteful dress disguising self-

loathing and the inability for young girls to understand and identify with substantive role models or a parent that cares. Instead, confused girls parade around as if they are Kim Kardashian, believing sexuality can replace an empty sense of self that's screaming to find "who am I."
-Dean Kalahar

Talent is God given- be humble
Fame is man given- be grateful
Conceit is self given- be careful -John Wooden

Whether you think you can, or you think you can't -you're right.
–Henry Ford

Never let failure get to your heart and never let success get to your head.
–Uncle Si, Duck Dynasty

If you want to change the world...
>Start off by making your bed
>Find someone to help you paddle
>Measure people by the size of their hearts, not the size of their flippers
>Get over being a sugar cookie and keep moving forward
>Don't be afraid of the circuses (extra work)
>Sometimes you have to slide down an obstacle head first
>Don't back down from the sharks
>You must be your very best in the darkest moments
>Start singing when you are up to your neck in mud
>Don't ever, ever ring the bell.

-William H. McRaven, 9th Commander, US Special Operations Command.

Charity

[With] charity as with everything else, it cannot simply be assumed that more is always better. A "safety net" can easily become a hammock.
–Thomas Sowell

Helping those who have been struck by unforeseeable misfortunes is fundamentally different from making dependency a way of life.
–Thomas Sowell

Charlatans

Charlatans are recognizable in that they will give you positive advice, and only positive advice, exploiting our gullibility and sucker-proneness for recipes that hit you in a flash as just obvious, then evaporate later as you forget them. Just look at the "how to" books with, in their title, "Ten Steps for—"–Shane Parrish

Christmas

Linus: Sure Charlie Brown, I can tell you what Christmas is all about. Lights please?

And there were in the same country shepherds, abiding in the field, keeping watch over their flock by night. And, lo, the angel of the Lord came upon them, and the glory of the Lord shone round about them! And they were sore afraid. And the angel said unto them, "Fear not! For, behold, I bring you tidings o great joy, which shall be to all my people. For unto you is born this day in the city of David a Saviour, which is Christ, the Lord. And this shall be a sign unto you: Ye shall find the babe wrapped in swaddling clothes, lying in a manger." And suddenly, there was with the angel a multitude of the Heavenly Host praising God, and saying, "Glory to God in the Highest, and on Earth peace, and good will toward men.

That's what Christmas is all about, Charlie Brown.
-Charles Schultz

Class warfare

Class warfare is now not about brutal elemental poverty of the sort Charles Dickens or Knut Hamsun once wrote about. It is too often the anger that arises from not having something that someone else has, whether or not such style, privilege, or discretionary choices are all that necessary. -Victor Davis Hanson

Civilization

There are far too many historic examples of institutions that evolved into powerful forces that undermined the very civilization they were built to sustain. -Dean Kalahar

If you are not prepared to use force to defend civilization, then be prepared to accept barbarism. -Thomas Sowell

Once the restraints of family, religion, popular culture, and public shame disappear, ever more insulated by our material things from danger, we lack all appreciation of the eternal thin veneer of civilization. -Victor Davis Hansen

Early Romans knew what it was to be Romans, why it was at least better than the alternative, and why the culture had to be defended. Later, in ignorance, they forgot what they knew, in pride mocked who they were, and, in consequence, disappeared. -Victor Davis Hansen

The culture of this nation is being dismantled, brick by brick, but so gradually that many will not notice until the walls start to sag -- just before they cave in. -Thomas Sowell

History gives evidence of no civilization that survived long as purely secular and without a god, that put its trust in reason alone, and believed human nature was subject to radical improvement given enough capital and learning invested in the endeavor. -Victor Davis Hansen

We can rebuild America to be, as Reagan said, "a shining city upon a hill whose beacon light guides freedom-loving people everywhere." If we, however, ignore the warnings and sow the seeds to our own destruction, as the Romans did long ago, our fate will be written in the epilogue of history. Gone, a nation whose torch was smothered when a complacent arrogance forgot what made them great, and the humility to stand vigilant in defending liberty was lost. -Dean Kalahar

Such is the tragi-comedy of our situation---we continue to clamor for those very qualities we are rendering impossible. In a sort of ghastly simplicity we remove the organ and demand the function. We make men without chests and expect of them virtue and enterprise. We laugh at honor and are shocked to find traitors in our midst. We castrate and bid the geldings be fruitful. -C.S. Lewis

I wish we could all just hold hands, get along and share lollipops while riding unicorns singing songs of peace and harmony. Ideals are so warm and fuzzy. Unfortunately we live in a world of natural laws, including human nature, scarcity, and competition to spread DNA and survive. Capitalism, limited republican government, the nuclear family, competitive education, and freedom of religion are the only hope of humanity. –Dean Kalahar

Where are we going? And why am I in this handbasket?! -Unknown

Just as the Europeans are stunned that their heaven on earth has left them weak and afraid, so too millions of Americans on the Left are angry that their own promised moral utopia is not so welcomed by the supposedly less educated and bright among them. But still, what drives Westerners, here and in Europe, to demand that we must be perfect rather than merely good, and to lament that if we are not perfect we are then abjectly bad—and always to be so unable to define and then defend their civilization against its most elemental enemies?

There has of course always been a utopian strain in both Western thought from the time of Plato's Republic and the practice of state socialism. But the technological explosion of the last 20 years has made life so long and so good, that many now believe our mastery of nature must extend to human nature as well. A society that can call anywhere in the world on a cell phone, must just as easily end war, poverty, or unhappiness, as if these pathologies are strictly materially caused, not impoverishments of the soul, and thus can be materially treated.

Second, education must now be, like our machines, ever more ambitious, teaching us not merely facts of the past, science of the future, and the tools to question, and discover truth, but rather a particular, a right way of thinking, as money and learning are pledged to change human nature itself. In such a world, mere ignorance has replaced evil as our challenge, and thus the bad can at last be taught away rather than confronted and destroyed.

Third, there has always been a cynical strain as well, as one can read in Petronius's Satyricon or Voltaire's Candide. But our loss of faith in ourselves is now more nihilistic than sarcastic or skeptical, once the restraints of family, religion, popular culture, and public shame disappear. Ever more insulated by our material things from danger, we lack all appreciation of the eternal thin veneer of civilization.

We especially ignore among us those who work each day to keep nature and the darker angels of our own nature at bay. This new obtuseness revolves around a certain mocking by elites of why we have what we have. Instead of appreciating that millions get up at 5 a.m., work at rote jobs, and live proverbial lives of quiet desperation, we tend to laugh at the schlock of Wal-Mart, not admire its amazing ability to bring the veneer of real material prosperity to the poor.

We can praise the architect for our necessary bridge, but demonize the franchise that sold fast and safe food to the harried workers who built it. We hear about a necessary hearing aid, but despise the art of the glossy advertisement that gives the information to purchase it. And we think the soldier funny in his desert camouflage and Kevlar, a loser who drew poorly in the American lottery and so ended up in Iraq—our most privileged never acknowledging that such men with guns are the only bulwark between us and the present day forces of the Dark Ages with their Kalashnikovs and suicide belts.

So we are on dangerous ground. History gives evidence of no civilization that survived long as purely secular and without a god, that put its trust in reason alone, and believed human nature was subject to radical improvement given enough capital and learning invested in the endeavor. The failure of our elites to amplify their traditions they received, and to believe them to be not merely different but far better than the alternatives, is also a symptom of crisis in all societies of the past, whether Demosthenes' Athens, late imperial Rome, 18th-century France, or Western Europe of the 1920s. Nothing is worse that an elite that demands egalitarianism for others but ensures privilege for itself. And rarely, we know, are civilization's suicides a result of the influence of too many of the poor rather than of the wealthy.–Victor Davis Hanson

Civil rights

Civil rights used to be about treating everyone the same. But today some people are so used to special treatment that equal treatment is considered to be discrimination. -Thomas Sowell

Liberals love to point to the civil rights advances of the 1960s as their trump card. But the desegregation of schools and other institutions began in the 1950s. The fact that the trend continued in the 1960s is hardly surprising. Nor was the economic rise of blacks a product of 1960s legislation. That rise was faster in the 1940s and 1950s than in the 1960s or afterward. The Civil Rights Act of 1964 and the Voting Rights Act of 1965 were important pieces of legislation. But a higher percentage of Republicans than of Democrats voted for these bills in both Houses of Congress. -Thomas Sowell

The evolution of the Voting Rights Act fits a familiar pattern... It starts out being about opportunity and ends up being about results.
-Abigail Thernstrom

"These Negroes," said alleged civil-rights hero Lyndon Baines Johnson, "they're getting pretty uppity these days, and that's a problem for us since they've got something now they never had before: the political pull to back up their uppity-ness. We've got to give them a little something — just enough to quiet them down, not enough to make a difference." So far, the LBJ plan seems to be working perfectly.
-Kevin Williamson via Ronald Kessler's "Inside The White House"

Black Americans did not leave the party of Lincoln for the party of Joe Biden; they left the party of Herbert Hoover for the party of Franklin Roosevelt. Or at least they thought they did. What they got instead was the party of sky-high crime, dangerous and dysfunctional schools, a joblessness rate for black men that is more than twice the rate for white men at 14 percent and rising. Twice the unemployment, twice the high-school dropouts, four times the abortions, four times the HIV, seven times the prison sentences, twelve times the babies born with congenital syphilis, fourteen times the murder victims, and nineteen times the gonorrhea.
-Kevin Williamson via Ronald Kessler's "Inside The White House"

Collusion

Price wars show that although collusion can occur between companies, the opposite is far more likely to take place because it is far easier for men to compete against one another than to trust each other.
-Dean Kalahar

Communism

I know that I am leaving the winning side for the losing side, but it is better to die on the losing side than to live under Communism.
- Whittaker Chambers

The irony of being a communist in a free country is always lost on the Howard Zinns of the world. – Bill Gallagher

Compassion

If society were to show compassion for every individual, it would have no standards. –Dennis Prager

People need to be fed, medicated, educated, clothed, and sheltered. If we're compassionate, we'll help them, but you get no moral credit for forcing other people to do what you think is right. There is great joy in helping people, but no joy in doing it at gunpoint." -Penn Jillette

What is more compassionate, being non-judgmental and culturally sensitive to a people's squalor or staunchly defending the principles that provide everyone with a dignified existence that includes food, clothing, shelter, freedom, liberty, and property? -Dean Kalahar

The irony is that those who wish to command the economy will promote their agendas as the most compassionate and humanistic while at the same time be hard at work building temples of inefficiency, the cost is the suffering of the masses to a degree that is cruel, yet unfortunately, not unusual by historical standards. -Dean Kalahar

If you want life saving economic growth and health, you must swallow the pill of empirical evidence. If you simply want to look like you care, shed tears of compassion and do-good intention. -Dean Kalahar

Economics stands in the way of what people have their hearts set on. -Thomas Sowell

When a goateed anarcho-syndicalist commits an act of vandalism at an anti-globalization protest, he might think that he's striking a blow against The Man, but he's really rallying against the chance some desperately poor little boy or girl has to live a healthier life. -Rich Lowry

Reformers ... decry "sweatshop labor" in Third World countries who export their products to the United States to be sold in American stores. Nothing is easier than to take cheap shots at those stores for "exploiting" Third World people- and nothing will hurt those Third World people more surely than losing one of their few meager opportunities to earn incomes by producing at lower costs than more fortunate people in more industrial countries. -Thomas Sowell

Competition

If competition has evils, it prevents greater evils. -John Stuart Mill

The question is how do you make money in a free market? You only make money if you can provide someone with something he or she is willing to pay for. You can't make money any other way. Therefore, in order to make money, you have to promote cooperation. You have to do something that your customer wants you to do. You don't do it because he orders you to. You don't do it because he threatens to hit you over the head if you don't. You do it because you offer him a better deal than he can get anywhere else. Now that's promoting cooperation. But there are other people who are trying to sell to him too. They're your competitors. So there is competition among sellers, but cooperation between sellers and buyers. -Milton Friedman

The case for free enterprise, for competition, is that it's the only system that will keep the capitalists from having too much power...The virtue of free enterprise capitalism is that it sets one businessman against another, and it's a most effective device for control. -Milton Friedman

We all win by some people temporarily losing. -Dean Kalahar

The very complexity of modern conditions makes competition the only method by which a coordination of affairs can be adequately achieved. -Friedrich Hayek

The outcomes of free competition force equality, while forcing equal outcomes replaces freedom with tyranny. -Dean Kalahar

So long as effective freedom of exchange is maintained, the central feature of the market organization of economic activity is that it prevents one person from interfering with another in respect of most of his activities. The consumer is protected from coercion by the seller because of the presence of other sellers with whom he can deal. The seller is protected from coercion by the consumer because of other consumers to whom he can sell. The employee is protected from coercion by the employer because other employers for whom he can work, and so on. And the market does this impersonally and without centralized authority.-Milton Friedman

Sometimes it doesn't matter that you have a better product, if your competitors have better salesmen. -Thomas Sowell

Conservation

Interestingly, those who believe the market creates the greatest efficiencies in protecting nature are considered conservationists because the market is focused on economizing or conserving scarce resources. Those who wish to use the government to legislate behaviors to protect nature can be considered environmentalists because they wish to command and control an environment of scarce resources. -Dean Kalahar

Conservatism

One of the pleasures of being a conservative is that you are always more or less pleased. Conservatives are pessimists, so when things go badly they have the pleasure of having their beliefs confirmed, and when they go well they enjoy the pleasant surprise. -George Will

Conservatives must object to values, not to individuals.-Dennis Prager

Conservatism is by nature a defensive posture. It is about protecting the constitutional system created by the Founders. But the creation of this constitutional arrangement was a revolutionary act. It provided a political framework to maximize individual freedom and allow citizens to exercise their talents and enjoy the best possible lives. What conservatism is about is freedom, and this is its natural unifying idea... The equality proposed by progressives and Democrats is a declaration of war on individual freedom, and therefore on the American constitutional framework. The steady erosion of that freedom is the consequence of progressives' political successes. ...The American republic was designed by its founders specifically to preserve individual freedom and to thwart the redistributive ambitions of the progressives of the day, ideals that are now referred to as "social justice." In the words of James Madison, these

included "a rage for paper money, for an abolition of debts, for an equal division of property, or for any other improper or wicked project." Freedom exists, Madison explained, only when the unequal endowments and unequal abilities of individuals — what he called their "diversity of faculties" — are respected and protected. This very diversity is the source "from which property rights originate" and "the protection of these faculties is *the first object of government*." Note that the first object of government is the protection of the *inequalities* that arise from the natural abilities and talents of its citizens — because government is instituted to guarantee the unalienable rights that constitute individual freedom…This freedom stands in the way of the progressive schemers. The idea of equality of results, which mobilizes, organizes, and inspires the Left, can be truly achieved only by the abolition of private property and the suppression of individual freedom. This is the real conflict that divides our nation between conservatives and progressives, between the defenders of freedom and its would-be destroyers. The progressive agenda is the systematic constriction of the realm of freedom — the private sector — and its replacement by the power of the state.
-David Horowitz

Constitution

The Constitution is not an instrument for the government to restrain the people, it is an instrument for the people to restrain the government.
-Thomas Jefferson

The Constitution is not a suicide pact.–Abraham Lincoln

The Constitution is the nation's fundamental law but is not the first law. The Declaration is, appearing on Page 1 of Volume 1 of the U.S. Statutes at Large, and the Congress has placed it at the head of the United States Code, under the caption, "The Organic Laws of the United States of America." Hence the Declaration "sets the framework" for reading the Constitution not as "basically about" democratic government — majorities — granting rights but about natural rights defining the limits of even democratic government. –George Will

Culture

Cultural inflation: When you artificially pump up the supply of something (whether it's currency or diplomas), the value drops. The reason why a bachelor's degree on its own no longer conveys intelligence and capability is that the government decided that as many people as possible should have bachelor's degrees. There's something of a pattern here. The government decides to try to increase the middle class by subsidizing things that middle class people have: If middle class people go to college and own homes, then surely if more people go to college and own homes, we'll have more middle class people. But homeownership and college aren't causes of middle-class status, they're markers for possessing the kinds of traits -- self-discipline, the ability to defer gratification, etc. -- that let you enter, and stay in, the middle class. Subsidizing the markers doesn't produce the traits; if anything, it undermines them. One might as well try to promote basketball skills by distributing expensive sneakers…If the government really wants to encourage people to achieve, and maintain, middle-class status, it should be encouraging things like self-discipline and the ability to defer gratification. -Glenn Reynolds

At one time cultural norms use to act as a filter for choices and behavior, today the filter has been removed. The stench of the self-absorbed is no longer an affront because society has gotten use to the smell of cultural rot. –Dean Kalahar

The reason that millions cross the Mediterranean to Europe or the Rio Grande to the United States is for something more that transcends the periphery and involves fundamental values — consensual government, free-market capitalism, the freedom of the individual, religious tolerance, equality between the sexes, rights of dissent, and a society governed by rationalism divorced from religious stricture. Somehow that obvious message has now been abandoned, as Western hosts lost confidence in the very society that gives us the wealth and leisure to ignore or caricature its foundations. …At just such a critical time, in our universities and bureaucracies, the pressures to assimilate in melting-pot fashion have been replaced by salad-bowl separatism — as if the individual can pick and choose which elements of his adopted culture he will embrace, which he will reject, as one might croutons or tomatoes. But ultimately he can do that because he senses that the American government, people, press, and culture reward such opportunism and have no desire, need, or ability to defend the very inherited culture that has given them the leeway to ignore it and so attracted others from otherwise antithetical paradigms. That is a prescription for cultural suicide. –Victor Davis Hanson

Defense

History's bleak lesson is that those societies with self-reliant citizens who protect themselves and their interests prosper; those whose citizens grow dependent cut back their defenses — and waste away.
-Victor Davis Hanson

When you enter a boxing ring, you agree to abide by the rules of boxing. But when you are attacked from behind in a dark alley, you would be a fool to abide by the Marquis of Queensbury rules. If you do, you can end up being a dead fool. -Thomas Sowell

We dare not tempt them with weakness. -John F. Kennedy

Jessup: You have no idea how to defend a nation. All you did was weaken a country today, Kaffee. That's all you did. You put people in danger. Sweet dreams, son. –A few Good Men, Movie

The decline of civilizations of the past — fourth-century-b.c. Athens, fifth-century-a.d. Rome, 15th-century Byzantium, 1930s Western Europe — was not caused by their spending too much money on defense or not spending enough on public entitlements. Rather, their expanding governments redistributed more borrowed money, while a dependent citizenry wanted even fewer soldiers so as to guarantee ever more handouts...History's bleak lesson is that those societies with self-reliant citizens who protect themselves and their interests prosper; those whose citizens grow dependent cut back their defenses — and waste away
-Victor Davis Hanson

Democracy

A democracy cannot exist as a permanent form of government. It can only exist until the voters discover that they can vote themselves largess from the public treasury. From that moment on, the majority always votes for the candidate promising the most benefits from the treasury with the result that a democracy always collapses over loose fiscal policy. -Alexander Tytler

In a pure democracy, "there is nothing to check the inducement to sacrifice the weaker party or the obnoxious individual. - James Madison

Remember, democracy never lasts long. It soon wastes, exhausts, and murders itself. There was never a democracy yet that did not commit suicide. -John Adams

Democracy encourages a taste for physical gratification; this taste, if it become excessive, soon disposes men to believe that all is matter only; and materialism, in its turn, hurries them on with mad impatience to these same delights; such is the fatal circle within which democratic nations are driven round. It were well that they should see the danger and hold back. -Alexis De Tocqueville

Diets

A diet is really a difficult thing to stick to; much more difficult than quitting smoking. With smoking we are either smokers or not smokers. With dieting, we can't separate ourselves into "eaters" and "non-eaters." We have to eat. -Dan Ariely

Discrimination

No matter who you are, if it is too costly to your profit margin to discriminate, you most likely will not, unless you like discrimination more than you like money. -Dean Kalahar

The way to stop discriminating on the basis of race is to stop discriminating on the basis of race. –Chief Justice John Roberts

If Latinos are underrepresented at the University of California, Berkeley; is it because of stubborn institutional prejudices, which, however, somehow have been trumped by Asian-Americans enrolling at three times their percentage of the state's general population? If women are so oppressed by men, why do they graduate from college in higher numbers than their chauvinist male counterparts? –Victor Davis Hanson

Diversity

Promoting "diversity" by segregation and discrimination -to end real or imagined bigotry- is not achieved by "embracing our differences," it is realized by focusing on our similarities. -Dean Kalahar

Promoting equality through diversity is like promoting a color-blind society by demanding we recognize race. -Dean Kalahar

You say that it is your custom to burn widows. Very well. We also have a custom: when men burn a woman alive, we tie a rope around their necks and we hang them. Build your funeral pyre; beside it, my carpenters will build a gallows. You may follow your custom. And then we will follow ours. -General Napier

According to the "diversity" ethos that prevails at America's elite universities, then, it is racist to make fun of people for their race but perfectly fine to discriminate on that basis. -James Taranto

A national language is a band of national union...for if we do not respect ourselves...other nations will not respect us. -Noah Webster

The minute you define some groups as protected from cruelty (bullying), you automatically make others candidates for it. -Catlin Flanagan

I have a dream: that a day will come when academics value diversity in the content of our minds, and not the color of our skin. - J. Storrs Hall

In terms of race and ethnicity, the classical-liberal tradition of emphasizing our character rather than our appearance has been eroded by the self-serving multiculturalism of our elites. Formal support for assimilation, intermarriage, and integration became passé, as hyphenation began to strain credulity, the "salad bowl" replaced the melting pot, and grand proclamations about the "other" became the new normal. Even as we intermarry and our popular culture blends us together, our elites tear us apart, distributing rewards and punishments in terms of jobs, entitlements, and education based on notions of difference. -Victor Davis Hanson

(We) have grown used to American institutions being so intimidated by the prospect of black wrath that they invent mushy ideas like "diversity" and "inclusiveness" simply to escape that wrath.
–Shelby Steele, The decline of the Civil Rights Establishment

Universities are no longer institutions of inquiry but 'safe spaces' where delicate flowers of diversity of race, sex, orientation, 'gender fluidity' and everything else except diversity of thought have to be protected from exposure to any unsafe ideas. –Mark Steyn

The voice of a generation: celebrate diversity by enforcing conformity. –Mark Steyn

Do-gooders

Do-gooders will always demand perfection and use examples showing the lack of utopia as evidence of wrong doing and the failure of capitalism. -Dean Kalahar

Do-gooders can sit in ivory towers directing decisions that are inefficient and lower the standard of living for those in the economy while paying no personal price for their grandiose schemes. -Dean Kalahar

Economics

Depth in economics consists in looking for all the consequences of a policy instead of merely resting one's gaze on those immediately visible. -Henry Hazlitt

The art of economics consists in looking not merely at the immediate but at the longer effects of any act or policy; it consists in tracing the consequences of that policy not merely for one group but for all groups. -Henry Hazlitt

Life does not ask what we want. It presents us with options. Economics is just one of the ways of trying to make the most of those options. -Thomas Sowell

Understanding economics is confusing, not understanding economics is costly. –Dean Kalahar

Economics is not about the financial fate of individuals. It is about the material well-being of society as a whole. -Thomas Sowell

Much of economics is a question of prices from central command vs. prices from supply and demand. -Dean Kalahar

Economics must not be relegated to classrooms and statistical offices and must not be left to esoteric circles. It is the philosophy of human life and action and concerns everybody and everything. It is the pith of civilization and of man's human existence. –Ludwig von Mises

There is only one difference between a bad economist and a good one: the bad economist confines himself to the visible effect; the good economist takes into account both the effect that can be seen and those effects that must be foreseen. -Frederic Bastiat

Economics is a theoretical science and as such abstains from any judgment of value. It is not its task to tell people what ends they should aim at. It is a science of the means to be applied for attainment of ends chosen, not, to be sure a science of choosing the ends. Ultimate decisions, the valuations and the choosing of ends are beyond the scope of any science. Science never tells a man how he should act; it merely shows how a man must act if he wants to attain definite ends. -Ludwig Von Mises

The curious task of economics is to demonstrate to men how little they really know about what they imagine they can design. -Friedrich Hayek

If ignorance paid dividends, most Americans could make a fortune out of what they don't know about economics. –Luther H. Hodges

I am for more economy, and after that I am for more economy.
-Calvin Coolidge.

"Buy American" hurts Americans. –Dean Kalahar

Economic Growth

Smaller Pie and People die. -Dean Kalahar

A rising tide lifts all boats. -John F. Kennedy

Economic growth throughout the system is hard to see but beneficial to all, while the economic pain and suffering of individuals is easy to see but detrimental to economic growth if acted upon in any substantial way. -Dean Kalahar

Economic growth is the engine that serves more without taking away from those who are already eating.-Dean Kalahar

Economic Lag

When the fool realizes that the water is too cold, he turns on the hot water. However, the hot water takes a while to arrive, so the fool simply turns the hot water up all the way, eventually scalding himself.
–Milton Friedman

Education

I know of no safe repository of the ultimate power of society but people. And if we think they're not enlightened enough, the remedy is not to take the power from them, but to inform them by education.
-Thomas Jefferson

Just as any village idiot can destroy a priceless Ming vase, so the shallow and fad-ridden people in our public schools can undermine and ultimately destroy a civilization that took centuries of effort and sacrifice to create and maintain.
-Thomas Sowell

American education needs to go back to the principles of classical economic and political theory for answers. Our schools need a counter-intuitive model that, like capitalism, works better than it sounds instead of continuing with a progressive model that sounds better than it works. –Dean Kalahar

If a nation expects to be ignorant and free, in a state of civilization, it expects what never was and never will be. -Thomas Jefferson

Too often what are called "educated" people are simply people who have been sheltered from reality for years in ivy-covered buildings. Those whose whole careers have been spent in ivy-covered buildings, insulated by tenure, can remain adolescents on into their golden retirement years. -Thomas Sowell

The education institution is feeding off its own ignorance, slowly destroying itself and the society it is supposed to support from within. -Dean Kalahar

Kids don't know what they don't know yet. –Anonymous

When educators believe the ends (power and dollars) justify the means (lying to the public who pay the bills), our cultural capital is being undermined by the very people charged with strengthening its foundation. In short, the education establishment is destroying the nation from within. -Dean Kalahar

The school is the unit that matters. Great schools often exist in spite of unsupportive, often intrusive, school district offices. –John White

After 50 years of undermining the social fabric of our nation, educators have created the very culture that makes educating children so difficult. The progressive education model has created a self fulfilling prophesy of geometrically increasing systemic failure. To paraphrase Senator Daniel Patrick Moynihan, schools have been the catalyst for "defining deviancy downward." In short, the more liberal educators push their worldview in schools, the more the culture corrodes, and the harder it is to teach kids who grow up in a dysfunctional world.

Until the addicts of progressive education admit they have a problem, they will continue to create at best, self-centered illiterates who feel entitled. At worst, they will all but destroy a great nation. Educators need a reality check of self-awareness to overcome their dissonance. -Dean Kalahar

Today, schools across the country are teaching students what to think---political correctness. Instead of knowledge, students are given "self-esteem," so that they can vent their ignorance with confidence. -Thomas Sowell

In the long run, the greatest weapon of mass destruction is stupidity. In an age of artificial intelligence, too many of our schools are producing artificial stupidity, in the sense of ideas and attitudes far more foolish than young people would have arrived at on their own. -Thomas Sowell

Of all the frauds which pervade the public schools, none is more hypocritical -- or more destructive -- than the pretense that they are trying to avoid the unfairness of subjecting disadvantaged children to standards and tests that they are not equipped to handle. What makes these people think that life will be any easier for the disadvantaged to handle? Certainly not when they are sent out into the world educationally unprepared and full of "self-esteem" that is going to have a brutal head-on collision with reality. -Thomas Sowell

Children should be educated and instructed in the principles of freedom. –John Adams

America's armed forces …do a far better job of shaping the minds and character of our youth than do our colleges. Somehow the military can take an 18-year-old and teach him to park a $100 million fighter on a carrier deck, but our colleges cannot ensure that his civilian counterpart will show up regularly for classes. –Victor Davis Hanson

More faculty now believe that they should teach their students to be agents of social change than believe that it is important to teach them the classics of Western civilization." -Peter Berkowitz

Scholarship, which is meant to be a bulwark of civilization against barbarism, is ever more frequently turned into an instrument of

rebarbarization." So lamented a wise man, half a century ago.
-Peter Nichols

We can't relive our youth but we certainly can help those who are in it.
–Dean Kalahar

In the so-called free society, individuals have the ability to succeed wonderfully but there is also equal potential to fail miserably. At our fingertips we have the capacity to learn all the teachings of Socrates, Plato, Aristotle, Buddha, Nietzsche, Kierkegaard, Jung, Freud and Maslow. But there is no demand for depth; all is superficial...There is greater demand for escaping into the self-created reality. -Kent Thune

When teachers see potential, students begin to respect themselves. Good teachers fill students with a belief that may or may not be justified. As children make the dangerous crossing from unproven belief to actual accomplishment, from potential to reality, a good teacher holds their hand so expertly that they don't even know their hand is being held. Students get better because a teacher tells them they're already better. It's that simple—a magic trick. And every success they'll have has some of this same magic in it, cultivated by the hands of a skilled teacher or by the generous trickery of the voice inside them a teacher instilled.
-David Duchovny, edited

Perfect students with perfect parents in a perfect society cannot learn things that they are not being taught. -Thomas Sowell

Teaching is both one of the hardest and one of the easiest jobs in the world, depending on how conscientiously it is done. It is also one of the noblest and one of the most corrupt occupations- again, depending on how it is done. -Thomas Sowell

Don't let school get in the way of your education. –Dan Pierce

Educators keep applying all the same faulty principles in their reform efforts that have already shown to be ineffective in educating children. In short, the very same people who created the education problems in the first place still believe that a round peg can fit into a square hole simply because they feel compassionately that it should. Sadly however, feelings don't teach kids how to read, write, and add. -Dean Kalahar

Great teachers love what they are teaching…You can't love something you don't know any more than you can love someone you don't know. – David McCullough

If the education principles, techniques, and reforms of the last 40 years have been a dismal failure, then would not the opposite principles, techniques and structure have to be successful? -Dean Kalahar

The successful education model: student interaction is guided by specific long term behaviors performed within a proper structure and guided by fundamental principles to accomplish goals. -Dean Kalahar

The reason the education institution has had such a difficult time reforming itself, or actually becoming more productive, is because intellectually inconsistent philosophies based more on feelings than reason make a mess of any hope for success. -Dean Kalahar

If educators don't face their beliefs and reactions, they no longer benefit from more experience. Such teachers may claim to have ten, twenty or thirty years of experience. What they really have is one year of experience thirty times. -Martin Haberman

In the zero-sum game of the education curriculum, each newly added therapeutic discipline eliminated an old classical one. The result is that if Americans emote more and have more politically correct thoughts on the environment, race, class, and gender, they are less able to advance their beliefs through fact-based knowledge. -Victor Davis Hanson

The Northwest Ordinance, adopted in 1787 and passed again in 1789, contains the following beautiful sentence: "Religion, morality, and knowledge, being necessary for good government and the happiness of mankind, the means of education shall forever be encouraged." Accordingly, Congress proceeded to give 1/36 of the land in the vast Northwest Territory—including Michigan and four other states—as an endowment, controlled by the states, to support education in each township. –Larry P. Arnn

The word "education" comes from a Latin word meaning "to lead forth." And if you think about it, "forth" is a value-laden term. Which way is

forth? The Bible tells us to "raise up a child in the way he should go."
But which way should he go? How does one come to know the answer to
that?.. I can tell you that if you ask a young person today which way is
the right way to go, more often than not he or she will answer: "It
depends on which way you want to go." Young people today give that
answer because they've been taught to give that answer. But it's the
wrong answer, and the activity of getting from there to the right
answer—the activity of coming to know which way is the right way—is
education. Thus "to lead forth." –Larry P. Arnn

We are supposed to believe that well-meaning teachers, who have spent
their entire time in ed school steeped in the doctrine of "white privilege"
and who are among the most liberal segments of the workforce, suddenly
become bigots once in the classroom and begin arbitrarily suspending
pacific black children out of racial bias. Oddly, the civil-rights industry
never accuses schools of being biased against boys, even though males
are as over-represented among disciplined students as blacks... Given the
black–white crime disparities, it is equally common sense that black
students are more likely to be disruptive in class as well.
–Heather McDonald

I'm not an educator who works to make the principal's job easy; I work
for the principles that make the job of education tough. –Dean Kalahar

Efficiency

Efficiency is getting the most out of the least for more people.
-Dean Kalahar

Scarcity forces us to make choices; efficiency is the degree to which we
make successful ones. -Dean Kalahar

J. A. Schumpeter used to refer to progress under capitalism as "creative
destruction" — the replacement of businesses that have outlived their
usefulness with businesses that carry technological and organizational
creativity forward, raising standards of living in the process.
-Thomas Sowell

They are called executives because they can execute the creation of efficiency. This is in contrast to public sector leaders who are called directors because they can orchestrate the creation of inefficiency.
-Dean Kalahar

Efficiency is the difference between having the necessities, comforts and amenities of high income countries and suffering the hunger and deprivations too often found in poor countries. -Thomas Sowell

The Soviet Union did not lack resources, but was in fact one of the most richly endowed nations on earth. What it lacked was an efficient economic system that made efficient use of scarce resources.
-Thomas Sowell

The story goes that Milton Friedman was once taken to see a massive government project somewhere in Asia. Thousands of workers using shovels were building a canal. Friedman was puzzled. Why weren't there any excavators or any mechanized earth-moving equipment? A government official explained that using shovels created more jobs. Friedman's response: "Then why not use spoons instead of shovels?"
–Russell Roberts

In August 1945, Hiroshima was in shambles, while Detroit was among the most innovative and wealthiest cities in the world. Contemporary Hiroshima now resembles a prosperous Detroit of 1945; parts of Detroit look like they were bombed decades ago. –Victor Davis Hanson

Employment

Just because a resource has feelings does not make conservation any less important. -Dean Kalahar

Most Americans earn their livings by renting their time and talents-and live much better than peoples in many other countries where most adults own their own land and work only for themselves. -Thomas Sowell

Environment

If man created global warming, then dinosaurs caused the ice age.
-Dean Kalahar

Some have no problem with beavers cutting down trees, damning rivers and altering the flow of streams with the death of many other animals as a result. However, they do have a problem if man cuts down trees, damns rivers, and alters the flow of streams with the death of many animals as a result. Some call this intellectual inconsistency; others call it hypocrisy to pretend to be what one is not. -Dean Kalahar

The environmental movement is a perfect vehicle. In today's America, it is the most natural place for someone with Marxist sensibilities and aspirations outside a college English department. A frontal assault on capitalism on behalf of the working people of the world is passé and doomed. A stealth assault on capitalism in the name of saving the planet is chic and entirely plausible. In this sense, green is the new red.
-Rich Lowery

CO2 from biological sources (animals, plants, fungi and microbes,) 800 billion tons a year. Total volcanic carbon dioxide emissions, 230 million tons a year. Fossil- fuel CO2 emissions, 32 billion tons a year. The scam of manmade global warming- priceless! –Dean Kalahar

If Freud were alive these days, he'd reduce their (environmentalists) psyche to the Id and the Super-eco. -James Lilek

It's a startling fact that "renewable" resources keep running short, while no non-renewable resource has yet run out: not oil, gold, uranium or phosphate. –Matt Ridley

The current environmental movement fixates on improvements that are immeasurable, intangible and unaffordable. Where earlier gains in environmental protection tangibly cleaned up dirty rivers, dirty lakes, and dirty air, it now fights against remote possibilities, against threats not actually visible...A movement that was both necessary and highly successful has become the reformer who can't stop reforming...A movement that began with rivers afire and moon views dyed brown by smothering smog has become a movement of hubris dictating the perfect climate and the perfect earth... Its mantra is a great "NO" proclaimed loudly and often. Its primary appeal is fear...Worse than any religion, it demands unquestioned loyalty, simply condemning those dissenting as ignorant or greedy... In a world that increasingly denies man his soul, it grants one to the earth at large. While it condemns conservatives for wanting a world of medieval simplicity, it longs for a world that predates man himself... we should be humbled by the thought that our world began as a geological composite of dead rock and bloomed into an orb teaming with life in every nook and cranny, on the land in the seas and in the air above, all without our help. To think it needs our micro-managing is hubris of the worst sort. It is a hubris that will ultimately regulate away both man's freedom and his humanity. -Victor Davis Hanson

I will start to worry about mans role in destroying the environment when fish stop pooping in the sea. –Dean Kalahar

Equality

Reducing global inequality as a principle of state action, however suggestive of an impeccable moral conscience, may well require curtailing fundamental rights underpinning free societies; free societies generally being one and the same with rich ones. Justice in a free society means treating individuals according to identical rules of conduct.
- From Benn Steil and Manuel Hinds, "Money, Markets, and Sovereignty" (2009)

Equivocating will never bring about equivalence, but "equivalency" is promoted by those who equivocate. –Dean Kalahar

A society that puts equality — in the sense of equality of outcome — ahead of freedom will end up with neither equality nor freedom. The use of force to achieve equality will destroy freedom, and the force, introduced for good purposes, will end up in the hands of people who use it to promote their own interests." -Milton Friedman

If the all-male military bastion is being eliminated, it stands to reason that prison segregation by sex should be eliminated. No decent American would accept the idea of a prison for blacks and another one for whites. If we value equality, we shouldn't accept one prison for men and another for women. There should be integration. –Walter Williams

Euphemisms

Lincoln Abraham once asked an audience how many legs a dog has, if you called the tail a leg? When the audience said "five," Lincoln corrected them, saying that the answer was four. "The fact that you call a tail a leg does not make it a leg. -Thomas Sowell

Evil

Evil hates good. –Dennis Prager

God neither wills moral evil to be done, nor wills that it not be done, but rather He "wills to permit evil to be done." – Aquinas

There is no safety for honest men, but by believing all possible evil of evil men, and by acting with promptitude, decision, and steadiness on that belief. -Edmund Burke

I think some people are unwilling to concede the evil exits in others because they view that's a concession that it must exist in all of us…If it does exist in everybody like certain people say, I'd say 99.999 have an ability to tamp it down. But the simple fact is there is good in the world, there is evil in the world, and when good can thin the evil heard you do; and if you're going over here and tell me the reasons we shouldn't and claim the moral high ground, I'm going to say that's immoral. -Dennis Miller

Facts

Facts don't speak for themselves, somebody has to articulate them. –Thomas Sowell

Fair

Fair is defined as freedom exercised as an agreement on an exchange. -Dean Kalahar

Fair' is in the eye of the beholder; free is the verdict of the market.
-Milton Friedman

Family

In every generation, Western civilization is invaded by barbarians — we call them children. -Hannah Arendt

A Viking baby magically transported to 21st-century America might grow up to be an accountant or a bus driver. A baby born today and sent back in time might become a Hun, Visigoth or Aztec warrior, whatever his parents expected of him. Families are civilization factories. They take children and install the necessary software, from what to expect from life to how to treat others. One hears a lot of platitudes about how children are "taught to hate." This is nonsense. Hating comes naturally to humans, and children are perfectly capable of learning to hate on their own. Indeed, everyone hates. The differences between good people and bad resides in what they hate, and why. -Jonah Goldberg

Raising children in the wild is far different than rearing them in a home. -Dean Kalahar

Pregnancy is a choice not an affliction. -Dean Kalahar

In a given year, the number of divorces may well be half as large as the number of marriages that year, but this is comparing apples to oranges. The marriages being counted are only those marriages taking place within a given year, while the divorces that year are from marriages that took place over a period of decades. To say that half of marriages end in divorce, based on such statistics, would be like saying that half of the population died last year if deaths were half as large as births. -Thomas Sowell

When it is easier to renounce a marriage than a mortgage and when parental notification is needed in order for a child to pierce their bodies, but is not necessary to have an abortion, the family institution is on shaky ground. -Dean Kalahar

The family institution has been redefined into a bizarre amalgam of gender, sexual, and parental proclivities. 40% of children are born out of wedlock and 25% of teenagers have a sexually transmitted disease. The overt-sexualization of our society has created confusion and despair among our children, while infanticide has become an all too easy choice. Biological and psychological realities for sanctioning marriage between a man and woman for the sake of their posterity have been ruthlessly attacked by those seeking to re-define the universal order. -Dean Kalahar

In the Old America there were a lot of bad parents. There always are, because being a parent is hard, and not everyone has the ability or even the desire. But in the old America you knew it wasn't so bad, because the culture could bring the kids up. Inadequate parents could sort of say, "Go outside and play in the culture," and the culture -- relatively innocent, and boring -- could be more or less trusted to bring the kids up. Popular songs, the messages in movies -- all of it was pretty hopeful, and, to use a corny old word, wholesome. Grown-ups now know you can't send the kids out to play in the culture, because the culture will leave them distorted and disturbed. And there isn't less bad parenting now than there used to be. There may be more. - Peggy Noonan

Today's adolescents develop an accelerator long time before they can steer and break. –Ronald Dahl

The wisdom of Solomon provided a good example many centuries ago, in a case where two women each claimed to be the mother of a child and each demanded custody. Since he did not know who the real mother was, King Solomon said that he would cut the child in half and give each mother her half. When one of the women dropped her claim in order to spare the child's life, he knew that she was the real mother. Anyone who would ruin a helpless child's life in order to assert her own legal prerogatives, or to protect the tribe's turf, raises very serious questions about what kind of parent she is. -Thomas Sowell

The family is the primary transmitter of social capital — the values and character traits that enable people to seize opportunities. Family structure is a primary predictor of an individual's life chances, and family disintegration is the principal cause of the intergenerational transmission of poverty. –George Will

By the time they are 15 or 16, twice as many children in Britain have a television as have a biological father living at home. The child may be father to the man, but television is father to the child. –Anthony Daniels

Fate

We would all do well to keep in mind: Sometimes, regardless of how diligently you prepare, or how splendidly you do your job, or how thoroughly you consider every aspect of the task, you get blindsided by fate. –Bob Greene

Feminism

[The] metamorphosis of liberated women into Victorian-era puritans was accompanied by yet another wild card: Sex was now everywhere. The old probity was gone. It was almost as if the more sexual suggestiveness became ubiquitous, the more we (the feminists) reverted to New England Puritanism. -Victor Davis Hanson

Most women don't want what the worst men have always wanted — sex with no strings attached. Women are all about strings. They want intimacy, tenderness, and commitment — all of which have been placed further out of reach by feminism's conquest of the culture.
–Mona Charen

Forgiveness

You forgive the person behind the act. You either do that, or your hate eventually consumes you. –Tim Townsend

We should forgive but don't have to reconcile. -Dean Kalahar

What people have done to you yourself, you can, if you like, forgive and forget. That is your own affair. But it (is) a terrible sin to burden your conscience (by forgiving) other people's sufferings. –Tim Townsend

The Bible has a very fitting and powerful word for those that harm children with no remorse or accountability, it says, "it is better for him to be thrown into the sea with a millstone tied around his neck. –Unknown

Freedom

The economic freedom which is the prerequisite of any other freedom cannot be the freedom from economic care which the socialists promise us and which can be obtained only by relieving the individual at the same time of the necessity and of the power of choice; it must be the freedom of our economic activity which, with the right choice, inevitably also carries the risk and the responsibility of that right. -Friedrich Hayek

There is no such thing as a free lunch. -Milton Friedman

In economics as elsewhere in life, while we are free to do whatever we wish, we are not free to have the consequences be whatever we want them to be. We can leap off the top of a skyscraper, if we wish, but the law of gravity will determine what the consequences will be. -Thomas Sowell

Those who wish for fairness without first protecting freedom will end up with neither freedom nor fairness. -Milton Friedman

I disapprove of what you say, but I will defend to the death your right to say it. –Voltaire

The tragic admission that we cannot be truly free if we are all forced to end up roughly equal against the idealism that if we are all roughly equal then we are at last truly free. –Victor Davis Hanson

The founders gave us freedom of religion not freedom from religion. -Dean Kalahar

The maintenance of a free society is a very difficult and complicated thing and it requires a self denying ordinance of the most extreme kind. It requires a willingness to put up with temporary evil on the basis of the subtle and sophisticated understanding that if you step in to do something about them, you not only may make them worse, but you will spread your tentacles and get bad results elsewhere. -Milton Friedman

Free Beer Tomorrow. –Sign

Freedom creates the best possible results for everyone in the long run, even if that means tolerating the worst of results for some in the short-run. -Dean Kalahar

One of There are instances of the abridgement of the freedom of the people by gradual and silent encroachments of those in power than by violent and sudden usurpations. -James Madison

Either human life is ennobled by the dangers and rewards of freedom or we are better off when governments baby-proof reality and shepherd us to the good. It is one way or the other, and history and reason must be brought to bear in order to determine which. –Andrew Klavin

The case for individual freedom rests chiefly on the recognition of the inevitable ignorance of all of us concerning a great many of the factors on which the achievement of our ends and welfare depends. -F.A. Hayek the wonderful things about America is that both the Left and Right are champions of freedom. The difference lies in what we mean by freedom. The Left emphasizes freedom as a material good, and the Right sees freedom as primarily a right rooted in individual sovereignty. For the Left, freedom means "freedom from want." If you don't have money, health care, homes, cars, etc., you're not free. Or as FDR put it when pitching his failed "Economic Bill of Rights": "Necessitous men are not free men." –Jonah Goldberg

When your response to everything that is wrong with the world is to say, 'there ought to be a law,' you are saying that you hold freedom very cheap. -Thomas Sowell

Freedom only extends to the tip of another man's nose. –Unknown

Son, we live in a world that has walls And those walls have to be guarded by men with guns. Who's gonna do it? You?.. I have a greater responsibility than you can possibly fathom. You weep for Santiago and you curse the marines. You have that luxury. You have the luxury of not knowing what I know: That Santiago's death, while tragic, probably saved lives. And my existence, while grotesque and incomprehensible to you, saves lives. You don't want the truth because deep down, in places you don't talk about at parties, you want me on that wall… (you need me on that wall). We use words like honor, code, loyalty...we use these

48

words as the backbone to a life spent defending something. You use 'em as a punch line. I have neither the time nor the inclination to explain myself to a man who rises and sleeps under the blanket of the very freedom I provide, then questions the manner in which I provide it. I'd prefer you just said thank you and went on your way. Otherwise, I suggest you pick up a weapon and stand a post. Either way, I don't give a d___ what you think you are entitled to. -A Few Good Men. (Movie)

The clash of ideas is the sound of freedom. -Unknown

Freedom- choice- cost

You can avoid the hangover costs of drinking if you just keep drinking. But you can't keep drinking forever. -Dean Kalahar via David Boaz

He may be a fool to drive that motorcycle without a helmet, but part of freedom ... is the freedom to be a fool. -Milton Friedman

Attaching the word "right" to any and all desires and then conferring an obligation upon another to meet the desire has nothing to do with freedom. -Dean Kalahar

Systemic choices trump elite absolutes because freedom trumps tyranny. -Dean Kalahar

Only God could have a free choice- and only on the first day of creation, since He would be confronted on the second day by what He had already done on the first. -Thomas Sowell

You can do anything you want; you just have to pay the consequences. -Dean Kalahar

The trouble with trouble is that it starts out looking like fun. –Unknown

To get the protection of the rules you have to play by the rules. -Thomas Sowell

Sometimes the road less traveled is less traveled for a reason. -Jerry Seinfeld

"I can't" means I choose not. –Unknown

If we don't make a decision, one will be made for us. -Thomas Sowell

When action is divorced from consequences, no one is happy with the outcome. –John Stossel

Free expression

(Muslim) Leaders who abuse and torture their own citizens for expressing their ideas or faith seem to think they have standing to lecture us about the limits of freedom. Well, the tribe of barbarism doesn't get to lecture the tribe of liberty about what freedom means. The thugs haranguing us about the proper limits of free expression aren't members of that tribe. They haven't paid their dues. –Jonah Goldberg

Free market

Market failures are different from the market being a failure. -Dean Kalahar

What we call the market is really a democratic process involving millions, and in some markets billions, of people making personal decisions that express their preferences. When you hear someone say that he doesn't trust the market, and wants to replace it with government edicts, they are really calling for is a switch from democratic to totalitarian processes. -Walter Williams

The free market is the check to the tyranny of business just like a free republic is a check to the tyranny of government. -Dean Kalahar

A free market economy is as much dependent on property rights as the political system is on free speech rights. -Thomas Sowell

Underlying most arguments against the free market is a lack of belief in freedom itself…The society that puts equality before freedom will end up with neither. The society that puts freedom before equality will end up with a great measure of both. . . The only way that has ever been discovered to have a lot of people cooperate together voluntarily is through the free market. And that's why it's so successful to preserving individual liberty. -Milton Friedman

Fundamentally, there are two ways of coordinating the economic activities of millions. One is central direction involving the use of coercion—the technique of the army and of the modern totalitarian state. The other is voluntary cooperation of individuals—the technique of the market place. -Milton Friedman

The free market creates incentives for individuals to make breakthroughs in technology for their own benefit and with ruthless disregard for the life saving consequences they pass on to the society as a whole. -Dean Kalahar

The only agenda the free market can promote is the efficient movement of scarce resources to their most valuable use by the effortless interplay of our friends, supply and demand. -Dean Kalahar

No one who buys bread knows whether the wheat from which it is made was grown by a Communist or a Republican, by a constitutionalist or a Fascist, or for that matter, by a Negro or a white. This illustrates how an impersonal market separates economic activities from political views and protects men from being discriminated against in their economic activities for reasons that are irrelevant to their productivity- whether these reasons are associated with their views or their color. The groups in our society that have the most at stake in the preservation and strengthening of competitive capitalism are those minority groups which can most easily become the object of distrust and enmity of the majority- . . .Yet, paradoxically enough, the enemies of the free market- the Socialists and Communists- have been recruited in disproportionate measure from these groups. Instead of recognizing that the existence of the market has protected them from the attitudes of their fellow countrymen, they mistakenly attribute the residual discrimination to the market. -Milton Friedman

The moral justification of the market process rests on the general prosperity and freedom it produces. -Thomas Sowell

In Britain, as elsewhere in medieval Europe, a "market" meant a specifically authorized gathering place for selling on days specified by the authorities, in places specified by the authorities, and at prices specified by authorities...As large scheduled markets and fairs gave way to innumerable, smaller, scattered, and continuously-operating shops and stores, official control of prices and conditions became much more tenuous as a practical matter...It was in the wake of these erosions of economic controls that intellectual challenges were then made to the role of government in the economy, first by the Physiocrats in France, who coined the term "laissez-faire," and then by Adam Smith in Britain, who became its leading champion. By the mid-nineteenth century, widespread support of "free trade" internationally, and of freeing the domestic economy from many political controls, were on the ascendancy in Britain. -Thomas Sowell

Free Speech

The point of free speech is for the stuff that's over the line, and strikingly unbalanced. If free speech is only for polite persons of mild temperament within government-policed parameters, it isn't free at all. –Mark Steyn

Once you get a taste for shutting people up, it's hard to stop. Why bother winning the debate when it's easier to close it down? –Mark Steyn

Free speech is essential to a free society because, when you deny people 'an opportunity to act like normal political parties', there's nothing left for them to do but punch your lights out. –Mark Steyn

Free speech buttresses the political system's legitimacy. It helps losers, in the struggle for public opinion and electoral success, to accept their fates. It helps keep them loyal to the system, even though it has disappointed them. They will accept the outcomes, because they believe they've had a fair opportunity to express and advance their views. There's always the next election. Free speech underpins our larger concept of freedom. –Robert Samuelson

Free speech and a dynamic, innovative society are intimately connected: a culture that can't bear a dissenting word on race or religion or gender fluidity or carbon offsets is a society that will cease to innovate, and then stagnate, and then decline, very fast. –Mark Steyn

It is not merely that, as the Big Climate enforcers say, 'the science is settled', but so is everything else, from abortion to gay marriage. –Mark Steyn

Friendship

Friends come and go but enemies accumulate. –Old Maxim

A brother may not be a friend, but a friend will always be a brother. -Benjamin Franklin

Perfect friendship is the friendship of men who are good, and alike in virtue…but it is natural that such friendships should be infrequent; for such men are rare. -Aristotle

Gambling

Risk, never gamble -Dean Kalahar

General Welfare

With respect to the two words 'general welfare' I have always regarded them as qualified by the denial of the powers connected to them. To take them in a literal and unlimited sense would be a metamorphosis of the Constitution. -James Madison

Congress has not unlimited powers to provide for the general welfare, but only those specifically enumerated. -Thomas Jefferson

Global Warming

Is it fair to use climate policies to keep poor people poor? Access to cheap and abundant power is one of the best ways to lift people out of poverty. Analyses show that there is a clear connection between growth and energy availability in Africa. Most spectacularly, China lifted 680 million people out of poverty over the past 30 years — not through expensive wind and solar, but through cheap, if polluting, coal…Nonetheless, many rich opinion leaders feel comfortable in declaring that the trade-off for cheap energy and development is not in the interest of the poor…. It seems immoral to me to want to reduce CO2 emissions through denying the very poorest energy access while we in the West continue to get more than two-thirds of our much higher energy consumption from fossil fuels. –Bjorn Lomborg, Roger Pielke and Daniel Sarewitz

Climate-change proponents have made their cause a matter of fealty and faith. For folks who pretend to be brave carriers of the scientific ethic, there's more than a tinge of religion in their jeremiads. If you whore after other gods, the Bible tells us, "the Lord's wrath be kindled against you, and he shut up the heaven, that there be no rain, and that the land yield not her fruit" (Deuteronomy 11). Today there's a new god, the Earth Mother. And a new set of sins — burning coal and driving a fully equipped F-150. But whoring is whoring, and the gods must be appeased. So if California burns, you send your high priest (in a carbon-belching Air Force One, but never mind) to the bone-dry land to offer up, on behalf of the repentant congregation, a $1 billion burnt offering called a "climate-resilience fund." –Charles Krauthammer

Climate policies take an even larger toll on people in the developing world. Almost three billion people rely on burning twigs and dung to cook and keep warm. This causes indoor air pollution, at the cost of 4.3 million lives a year, and creates the world's biggest environmental problem.

Access to cheap and plentiful electricity is one of the most effective ways out of poverty — curtailing indoor air pollution and allowing refrigeration to keep food from spoiling (and people from starving). Cheap electricity charges computers that connect the poor to the world. It powers agriculture and businesses that provide jobs and economic growth. The rich world generates just 0.8 per cent of its energy from solar and wind, far from meeting even minimal demand… Africa is the renewable utopia, getting 50 per cent of its energy from renewables — though nobody wants to emulate it.

In 1971, China derived 40 per cent of its energy from renewables. Since then, it has powered its incredible growth almost exclusively on heavily polluting coal, lifting a historic 680 million people out of poverty. Today, China gets a trifling 0.23 per cent of its energy from unreliable wind and solar. Yet most Westerners still want to focus on putting up more inefficient solar panels in the developing world. But this infatuation inflicts a real cost. A recent analysis from the Centre

54

for Global Development shows that $10 billion invested in such renewables would help lift 20 million people in Africa out of poverty. It sounds impressive, until you learn that if this sum was spent on gas electrification it would lift 90 million people out of poverty. So in choosing to spend that $10 billion on renewables, we deliberately end up choosing to leave more than 70 million people in darkness and poverty.
-Bjørn Lomborg

One-third of the world's people — 2.9 billion — cook and keep warm burning twigs and dung, which give off deadly fumes. This leads to strokes, heart disease and cancer, and disproportionately affects women and children. The World Health Organization estimates that it killed 4.3 million people in 2012. Add the smaller death count from outdoor pollution, and air pollution causes one in eight deaths worldwide. Compare these numbers to global warming... Air pollution doesn't garner the headlines afforded to global warming because it's not nearly as sexy. It's old-fashioned, boring, and doesn't raise anywhere near as much money as climate change. -Bjorn Lomborg

Going green

The green revolution has an entirely different meaning to most people in the affluent nations of the privileged world than to those in the developing nations of the forgotten world. -Norman Borlaug

The green movement claims to speak on behalf of consumers who don't know the light bulb ban is for their own good – if only they were more enlightened, as it were... But the iPhone wasn't created because the government regulated out of existence rotary phones and switchboards. Wait until congress decides to outlaw the internal combustion engine.
–Wall Street Journal, 2011

Government

Government isn't what you love if you're American, America is what you love. Government is what you have, need and hire. Its most essential duties—especially when it is bankrupt—involve defending rights and safety, not imposing views and values. We already have values.
–Peggy Noonan

Government involvement in economic matters creates the incentives for uncompetitive businesses to seek an edge they can't find in the marketplace. -Dean Kalahar

Government is the ultimate repository of force in a society. That force can be used to see that a general framework of laws is followed and that contracts between private individuals are enforced. This is basically an umpire's role. Free market economists are against the government being a player-umpire. In some sports there are player-managers but in no sports are there player-umpires. The two roles are incompatible. -Thomas Sowell

Government interventions create unintended consequences that lead to calls for further intervention, and so on into a destructive spiral of more and more government control. -Ludwig von Mises

Government is not reason; it is not eloquence. It is force. And force, like fire, is a dangerous servant and a fearful master. -George Washington

The question before the human race is whether the God of nature shall govern the world by its own laws, or whether priests and kings shall rule it by fictitious miracles. -John Adams

When buying and selling are controlled by legislation, the first things to be bought and sold are legislators. –P.J. O'Rourke

Little else is requisite to carry a state to the highest degree of opulence from the lowest barbarism but peace, easy taxes, and a tolerable administration of justice: all the rest being brought about by the natural course of things. All governments which thwart this natural course, which force things into another channel, or which endeavour to arrest the progress of society at a particular point, are unnatural, and to support themselves are obliged to be oppressive and tyrannical. –Adam Smith

The argument is between conservatives who say U.S. politics is basically about a condition, liberty, and progressives who say it is about a process, democracy. Progressives, who consider democracy the source of liberty, reverse the Founders' premise, which was: Liberty preexists governments, which, the Declaration says, are legitimate when "instituted" to "secure" natural rights. Progressives consider, for example, the rights to property and free speech,... "spaces of privacy" that government chooses "to carve out and protect" to the extent that these rights serve democracy. Conservatives believe that liberty, understood as a general absence of interference, and individual rights, which cannot be exhaustively listed, are natural and that governmental restrictions on them must be as few as possible and rigorously justified. Merely invoking the right of a majority to have its way is an insufficient justification. –George Will

Government spending

I place economy among the first and most important virtues, and public debt as the greatest of dangers to be feared. To preserve our independence, we must not let our rulers load us with perpetual debt. If we run into such debts, we must be taxed in our meat and drink, in our necessities and in our comforts, in our labor and in our amusements. If we can prevent the government from wasting the labor of the people, under the pretense of caring for them, they will be happy.
-Thomas Jefferson

And I sincerely believe, with you, that banking establishments are more dangerous than standing armies; and that the principle of spending money to be paid by posterity, under the name of funding, is but swindling futurity on a large scale. -Thomas Jefferson

We must not let our rulers load us with perpetual debt. We must make our selection between economy and liberty or profusion and servitude. If we run into such debts as that we must be taxed in our meat in our drink, in our necessities and comforts, in our labors and in our amusements, for our callings and our creeds... private fortunes are destroyed by public as well as by private extravagance. -Thomas Jefferson

We have tried spending money. We are spending more than we have ever spent before and it does not work. -Henry Morgenthau, Secretary of the Treasury under President Franklin D. Roosevelt

Cutting the budget will inhibit our ability to cut the budget. –politician

The Left's focus on the status of wealthy and high-income Americans is precisely backward — backward if improving the lives and opportunities of those born into poverty is your goal. If your goal is to increase the income and power of the public sector for your own economic and political ends, then of course it makes more sense to focus on the rich: That's where the money is, and the perverse reality of the Left is that it cannot fortify its own interests by improving the lives of the poor but can do so by pillaging the rich.

Indeed, a generation of transformative economic dynamism for the worst-off Americans would be a political and cultural catastrophe for the Left, whose power has its foundation in those who are to some extent dependent upon government largesse and — much more important — those who make their careers managing that dependency.

A lesson that conservatives keep not quite managing to learn is that our long-term problem is not so much those who are receiving checks from the government as it is those who are signing them. Economically rational people who are dependent upon government support can be weaned from it through the relatively simple expedient of a better deal; economically rational people who are in the employ of the welfare bureaucracies at above-market wages are not expecting a better deal, nor should they be. –Kevin Williamson

Greed

Greed for money is far different than greed for power. - Dean Kalahar

Some people consider it a valid criticism of corporations that they are just in the business to make profits. By this kind of reasoning, workers are just working to earn their pay. -Thomas Sowell

The greed of the seller is cancelled out by the greed of the buyer.
-Dean Kalahar

Blaming economic disasters on greed is like blaming gravity for airplane disasters. -Steve Forbes

If everybody is greedy, then the word is virtually meaningless.
-Thomas Sowell

Amid all the media hysteria over the price of gasoline and the profits of "Big Oil," one simple fact has been repeatedly overlooked: The oil companies' earnings are just under 10 percent of the price of a gallon of gas, while taxes take 17 percent. Yet who ever accuses the government of "greed"? -Thomas Sowell

It means zero to be against greed. Greed is a basic part of animal nature. Being against it is like being against breathing or eating. It means nothing. -Ben Stein

Among the many other questions raised by the nebulous concept of "greed" is why it is a term applied almost exclusively to those who want to earn more money or to keep what they have already earned-never to those wanting to take other people's money in taxes or to those wishing to live on the largess dispenses from such taxation. -Thomas Sowell

To say that prices are due to greed is to imply that sellers can set prices by an act of will. If so, no company would go bankrupt, since it could simply raise its prices to cover whatever costs happened to be. -Thomas Sowell

Businessmen work for money because money gives them mastery over their own lives. Politicians work for power because power gives them mastery over the lives of others. -P.J. O'Rourke

Greed for wealth saves lives. Greed for power; a.k.a. fraud, theft, dishonesty, lobbying, looting, plundering, and enslaving -kills. -Dean Kalahar

"For where your treasure is, your heart will be also," said Jesus Christ. A pedestrian reduction of the Son of God's saying is: Follow the money. -George Neumayr

Our current woes could not have been caused by "greed", because human nature is a constant. – Louis Woodhill

Greed = enlightened self-interest. –Walter Williams

People in the education and political establishments pretend they're not motivated by such "callous" motives as greed and profits. These people "care" about us, but from which areas of our lives do we derive the greatest pleasures and have the fewest complaints, and from which areas do we have the greatest headaches and complaints? We tend to have a high satisfaction level with goods and services like computers, cell phones, movies, clothing and supermarkets. These are areas where the motivations are greed and profits. Our greatest dissatisfaction is in areas of caring and no profit motive such as public education, postal services and politics. Give me greed and profits, and you can keep the caring.
- Walter E. Williams

We simply don't mind that Google and Amazon rake in billions, but we despise Exxon and Archer Daniels Midland for doing the same. It is not that we need social networking and Internet searches more than food and fuel, but rather that we have the impression that cool zillionaires in flip flops are good while un-cool ones in wingtips are quite bad.
–Victor Davis Hanson

Greed in moderation is called ambition. –Unknown

Happiness

How rich you are has very little to do with how much money you have in the bank and a lot to do with your expectations of what you need that money to do for you. It's a two-part equation, and a lot of people become miserable ignoring the second part... A person who makes $50,000 a year but only needs $30,000 to be happy is much richer than the person who makes $1 million but needs $1.1 million. –Morgan Housal

Harassment

The presumption that reckless men are criminals but reckless women are victims makes a mockery of any notion that the sexes are equal.
-James Taranto

Hate crimes

People who glibly talk about "hate crimes" ignore both the past and the implications for the future in what they are advocating. It took centuries of struggle and people putting their lives on the line to get rid of the idea that a crime against "A" should be treated differently than the same crime committed against "B." After much sacrifice and bloodshed, the principle finally prevailed that killing a peasant deserved the same punishment as killing a baron. Now the "hate crime" advocates want to undo all that and take us back to the days when punishment did not fit the crime, but varied with who the crime was committed against. -Thomas Sowell

History

You can't change history, you can only make history. -Dean Kalahar

Dwell on the past and you'll lose an eye. Forget the past and you'll lose both eyes. –Proverb

When the past no longer illuminates the future, the spirit walks in darkness. – Tocqueville

The study of history is a powerful antidote to contemporary arrogance. It is humbling to discover how many of our glib assumptions, which seem to us novel and plausible, have been tested before, not once but many times and in innumerable guises; and discovered to be, at great human cost, wholly false. -Paul Johnson

The 19th century was the age of production, the 20th century was the age of consumption, and the 21st century is the age when the consumer has become the product, a demographic statistic sold to advertisers. –Henry Allen

Hubris

For the ancient Greeks, hubris described the sort of arrogance that offends the gods and precedes the fall. –Jonah Goldberg

Human nature

Don't assume man is good because man does "good." –Dean Kalahar

We don't get angry over gravity, so why get upset about human nature. -Dean Kalahar

We all have what theologians call a "fallen" nature and no one should judge himself morally superior to others. But that does not mean the standard for "right" behavior should be eliminated simply because many appear unwilling to conform to that standard. -Cal Thomas

As long as we are aware of the evil nature that lurks just beneath the surface, we are capable of good. If we believe we are good, while forgetting what lurks beneath the surface, only evil will result. -Dean Kalahar

At some point everyone risks buying his own myth. -Kathleen parker

The founders of a new colony, whatever Utopia of human virtue and happiness they might originally project, have invariably recognized it among their earliest practical necessities to allot a portion of the virgin soil as a cemetery, and another as the site of a prison. -Nathaniel Hawthorne

It is indeed probable that more harm and misery have been caused by men determined to use coercion to stamp out a moral evil than by men intent on doing evil. -Friedrich Hayek

Human sin is constant, none are free, and anyone who is shocked by it is a fool or lying. –Peggy Noonan

The better angels of our nature. –Abraham Lincoln

Inhumanity, like humanity, is universal. -Thomas Sowell

There is no safety for honest men, but by believing all possible evil of evil men, and by acting with promptitude, decision, and steadiness on that belief. -Edmund Burke

Man can only create a best case scenario based on his human limits which is most certainly not a utopia. -Dean Kalahar

Many now believe Let us suppose the Great Wall of China, with all its myriads of inhabitants, was suddenly swallowed up by a earthquake, and let us consider how a man of humanity in Europe, who had no sort of connexion with that part of the world, would be affected upon receiving intelligence of this dreadful calamity. He would, I imagine, first of all, express very strongly his sorrow for the misfortune of that unhappy people, he would make melancholy reflections upon the precariousness of human life, and the vanity of all the labours of man, which could be annihilated in a moment. He would too, perhaps, if he was a man of speculation, enter into many reasonings concerning the trade and business of the world in general. And when all this fine philosophy was over, when all these humane sentiments had been once fairly expressed, he would pursue his business or his pleasure, take his repose or his diversion, with the same ease and tranquility, as if no such accident had happened. The most frivolous disaster which could befall himself would occasion a more real disturbance. -Adam Smith

No man knows how bad he is until he has tried to be good. -C.S. Lewis

Remembering the Rwanda genocide of 1994 that killed 500,000-800,000 in the span of 100 days provides a sobering example of the effects that human nature coupled to balkanized nations can manifest. -Dean Kalahar

That thought of the perfectibility of the human condition, in lieu of deterrence and military preparedness, throughout history has gotten millions killed. The human condition can be improved, but only by acknowledgment of the lethal propensities of some and by readiness to prevent those propensities' becoming manifest. Most of the great wars of the 20th century were fought against those who were convinced that "the human condition can be perfected." -Victor Davis Hanson

Neither individuals nor companies are successful forever.
-Thomas Sowell

Success has a half life. -Dean Kalahar

Men who don't benefit from their hard work tend not to work very hard. -David Boaz

(President Bill) Clinton told one last story, about hunting for lost golf balls with his dogs. On walks near his home in New York's Westchester County, he frequently heads for a part of the woods that borders a private golf course. "I don't know why I do this, because Lord knows I have all the golf balls I can use and the money now to buy more. But I take a little basket with me, and a tool to clean off the balls we find. I've got at least a hundred now," he said with a laugh. "It reminds me of when I was 12." –John Paul Newport

The self-absorption of human nature knows no bounds. People will gnaw away on you like piranhas. –Dean Kalahar

The construction of a theoretical paradise is the easiest of human efforts. The familiar method is to establish the perfect or almost perfect state, and then to fashion human beings to fit it. This is a far lighter undertaking the necessary and unspectacular task, taking human nature as it is and is likely to remain, of contriving improvements that are workable. -George W. Liebmann

The instinctive attraction of tribalism endures. The same drives that once pushed tribes to kill the villagers downriver still reside in us. We've just learned to channel and check them better. Bowling leagues, football franchises, high-school rivalries, motorcycle clubs… but underneath them all is the instinctual tribal refusal to let marauders tear down what we've built. –Jonah Goldberg

Ninety-five percent of what people say about you is going to be negative. And remember, that means that you are doing a good job. –Scott Boras

We should not confuse material progress with moral advancement. Just because Boko Haram members have cell phones and AK-47s does not mean that they have evolved much from their predecessors' days of whips and chains. And just because the sultan of Brunei flies in private jets does not mean that his worldview is any different from that of his forefathers who on horseback enforced the same sharia law. –Victor Davis Hanson

Humility

Humility is not thinking less of yourself; it is thinking of yourself less. -C.S. Lewis

Ideologies

Political ideologies are fairy tales for adults. -Thomas Sowell

Immigration

A nation's government that allows open borders and protects illegal workers by either not passing or enforcing citizenship and property laws is allowing the exploitation of humans. -Dean Kalahar

The immigrant malcontent: "Please do not send me back to the culture I nostalgically praise; please let me stay in the culture that I ignore or deprecate." – Victor Davis Hanson

Anyone can become in spirit an American, even before coming to these shores. Americans may choose to live in France or China, but we never become French or Chinese; but anyone can become fully American, simply by embracing our principles- and also by swearing allegiance to the flag and to the republic for which it stands. – Amy & Leon Kass

Incentives

Incentives, however negatively self-interested they seem to be, act as great motivators for individuals to do great things for the benefit of others whom they do not know. -Dean Kalahar

Incentives drive behavior, good intentions do not. -Dean Kalahar

Hit a dog with a stick, and you won't know where to find him. Leave him a bowl of food and you can be sure to know where he is. -Arthur Laffer

Cars travel faster because they have brakes. -Joseph Schumpeter

People aren't "good" or "bad." People are people, and they respond to incentives. They can nearly always be manipulated- for good or ill- if only you find the right levers. -Steven D. Levitt

Inflation

Inflation yields revenue to the government . . . by paying off-or repudiating, if you will-part of the government's debt. Government borrows in dollars and pays back in dollars. But thanks to inflation, the dollars it pays back can buy less than the dollars it borrowed.
-Milton Friedman

As it has become politically less attractive to vote higher taxes to pay for higher spending, legislators have resorted to financing spending through inflation, a hidden tax that can be imposed without having been voted, taxation without representation. -Milton Friedman

A society that values price level stability should not entrust the control of its money to people who benefit from inflation. -H.D. Thoreau

When prices fall as a result of productive processes and technical apparatus, that is called progress. Bad deflation is when merchants, drowning in debt and unable to get credit, dump goods at fire-sale prices.
-James Grant

Innovative companies and jobs are a function of investment, but when money is being devalued investment in the intellectual concepts that actually grow the economy lose out in favor of inflation hedges.
–John Tamny

The dollar has lost more than 98% of its value since the Federal Reserve. It was valued at a 20.67th of an ounce of gold back then. Today it is valued at less than a 1,200th of an ounce of gold. It has lost more than 34% of its value since President Obama was sworn to the presidency.
-Editorial, New York Sun, 5/2/2014

Innovation

Greater consumption due to increase in population and growth of income heightens scarcity and induces price run ups. A higher price represents an opportunity that leads inventors and business people to seek new ways to satisfy the shortages. Some fail, at cost to themselves. A few succeed, and the final result is that we end up better off than if the original shortage had never arisen. That is, we need our problems, though this does not imply that we should purposely create additional problems for ourselves. -Julian Simon

The great advances of civilization, whether in architecture or painting, in science or literature, in industry or agriculture, have never come from centralized government...Newton and Leibnitz; Einstein and Bohr; Shakespeare, Milton, and Pasternak; Whitney, McCormick, Edison, and Ford; Jane Addams, Florence Nightingale and Albert Schweitzer; no one of these opened new frontiers in human knowledge and understanding, in literature, in technical possibilities, or in the relief of human misery in response to governmental directives. Their achievements were the product of individual genius, of strongly held minority views, of social climate permitting variety and diversity. -Milton Friedman

The Stone Age did not end for a lack of stone.
–Sheikh Ahmed Zaki Yumanni

The idea of a Chinese-invented Google is a paradox, a Russian Facebook a joke, a Japanese-inspired Wal-Mart impossible. -Victor Davis Hanson

Everything is amazing and nobody is happy. We complain about airport delays and flying but do not realize "you're sitting in a chair in the sky."
–Louis C.K.

The perfect world will be found in neither poverty nor prosperity. But one is better than the other. Prosperity will always be messy. There will always be accidents waiting to happen and unforeseen consequences. However, history shows — particularly the history of the United States — that more people live better lives when they are willing to take those risks and deal with the consequences as they occur...Don't make the perfect the enemy of the good. –Mark Stein

Integrity

If you have integrity, nothing else matters. If you don't have integrity, nothing else matters. -Alan K. Simpson

Intelligence

This is perhaps the assembly of the most intelligence ever to gather at one time in the White House with the exception of when Thomas Jefferson dined alone. -John F. Kennedy

He who knows only his own side of the case, knows little of that.
- John Stuart Mill

Intentions

The good intentions of Dr. Frankenstein to engineer a superior life form lead to monstrous results. -Dean Kalahar

Good intentions do not make bad acts less wrong. -Marianne Jennings

The road to hell is paved with good intentions.
–Proverb, Saint Bernard of Clairvaux, John Ray

Interdependence

Interdependence is one of those academic buzzwords that is as universally appealing and nutritious as popcorn. -Ed Patterson

Investment

Compound interest is the most powerful force in the universe.
–Albert Einstein

Invisible hand

He generally, indeed, neither intends to promote the public interest, nor knows how much he is promoting it. By preferring the support of domestic to that of foreign industry, he intends only his own security;

and by directing that industry in such a manner as its produce may be of the greatest value, he intends only his own gain, and he is in this, as in so many other cases, led by an invisible hand to promote an end which was no part of his intention. Nor is it always the worse for the society that it was no part of. By pursuing his own interest he frequently promotes that of the society more efficiently than he really intends to promote it. -Adam Smith

The produce of the soil maintains at all times nearly that number of inhabitants which it is capable of maintaining. The rich only select from the heap what is most precious and agreeable. They consume little more than the poor, and in spite of their natural selfishness and rapacity, though they mean only their own conveniency, through the sole end which they propose from the labours of all the thousands whom they employ, be the gratification of their own vain and insatiable desires, they divide with the poor the produce of all their improvements. They are led by an invisible hand to make nearly the same distribution of the necessaries of life, which would have been made, had the earth been divided into equal portions among all its inhabitants, and thus without intending it, without knowing it, advance the interests of the society, and afford means to the multiplication of the species. -Adam Smith

Justice

Mercy to the guilty is cruelty to the innocent. –Adam Smith

I never ask for mercy, but I do ask for avoidance of injustice. –Conrad Black

If we are to supplement or replace the classical principle of justice, which applies to individual conduct, with one of global "social justice"— or more precisely, "distributive justice"—wherein no one shall acquire more benefits than a designated authority deems justified by the prevailing distribution of global wealth, the authority will of necessity need to treat individuals according to vastly different rules of conduct. -Benn Steil and Manuel Hinds, "Money, Markets, and Sovereignty" (2009)

Karma

Nemesis, remember, is not just karma, but payback with an absurd twist.
–Victor Davis Hanson

Keynesianism

Regarding Keynesian economics, "If you increase demand, prices go up. If you increase supply -as Reagan did- prices go down." –Steven Moore

It is our nature to always demand things. As such governments should never concern themselves with a lack of it. As humans our wants are unlimited. -John Tamny

Knowledge

Horses are supposed to be dumb animals. But they are smart enough not to bet on people. -Thomas Sowell

A fool can put on his coat better than a wise man can put it on for him. -Unknown

People are all born ignorant but they are not born stupid. -Thomas Sowell

Facts are stubborn things. -John Adams

None of us is as smart as all of us. –Japanese proverb

Someone once said that an idea that fails repeatedly may possibly be wrong. -Thomas Sowell

The only thing I know is that I know nothing. –Socrates

Man can create all sorts of utopias in the mind but in the end we will be pitting ourselves against an order in which we do not even have the most basic understanding. -Dean Kalahar

It may indeed prove to be far the most difficult and not the least important task for human reason rationally to comprehend its own limitations. It is essential for the growth of reason that as individuals we should bow to forces and obey principles which we cannot fully hope to understand, yet on which the advancement and even preservation of civilizations depend. -Friedrich A. Hayek

Those who can make you believe absurdities can make you commit atrocities. -Voltaire

Some people are so busy being clever that they don't have time enough to be wise. -Thomas Sowell

When we study the effects of various proposals, not merely on special groups in the short run, but on all groups in the long run, the conclusions we arrive at usually correspond with those of unsophisticated common sense. -Henry Hazlitt

Endless repetition does not make something true. -Thomas Sowell

Vague and mysterious forms of speech, and abuse of language, have so long passed for mysteries of science; and hard or misapplied words with little or no meaning have, by prescription, such a right to be mistaken for deep learning and height of speculation, that it will not be easy to persuade either those who speak or those who hear them, that they are but the covers of ignorance and hindrance of true knowledge
-John Locke

Herein is the evil of ignorance, that he who is neither good nor wise is nevertheless satisfied with himself. –Plato

Arrogance is no substitute for experience. –Thomas Sowell

On the battlefield of ideas, winning requires moving toward the sound of the guns. -Newt Gingrich

Some may know a lot about a little, but you all know a little about a lot more. -Dean Kalahar

Hindsight is not wisdom. -George W. Bush

Just because something is a paradox does not make it wrong.
-Dean Kalahar

It is much easier to dismiss your opponents as driven by mysterious forces than do the hard work of developing arguments built on human reason. -John Yoo

Stupid is as stupid does. -Forrest Gump (movie)

Being smart is what keeps some people from being intelligent
-Thomas Sowell

Intellectuals love complexity because they detest moral absolutes, conviction, and consequences. -Marianne Jennings

You want answers? I think I'm entitled to them. You want answers?! I want the truth. You can't handle the truth! -A few good men (movie)

Contrarianism is creativity for the unwise. -Dennis Miller

He that thinks himself the happiest is really so, but he that thinks himself the wisest is generally the greatest fool. -Francis Bacon

The dumb think they are smart because they are so dumb they don't even know how dumb they are. -Dean Kalahar

The risk is not in what he does not know but in what he thinks he knows.
-Rousseau

Considering the enormous range of human knowledge, from intimate personal knowledge of specific individuals to the complexities of organizations and the subtleties of feelings, it is remarkable that one speck in this firmament should be the sole determinant of whether someone is considered knowledgeable or ignorant, however much he may know about nature and man, and a Ph.D. is never considered ignorant, however barren his mind might be outside his narrow specialty and however little he grasps about human feeling or social complexities.
-Thomas Sowell

Reading furnishes the mind only with materials for knowledge; it is thinking that makes what we read ours...till a man can judge whether they be truths or not, his understanding is but little improved, and thus men of much reading, though greatly learned, but may be of little knowing. -John Locke

Realizing your own stupidity could be the smartest thing you've ever done. -Mike Alexander

Ignorance is easy. -Dean Kalahar

Believing does not make it the truth. -Dean Kalahar

Everyone is entitled to his own opinion, but not his own facts. -Daniel Patrick Moynihan

Nothing in the world is more dangerous than a sincere ignorance or a conscientious stupidity. -Martin Luther King Jr.

When John Stuart Mill was a young man, he worried that we were running out of music, since there were only 8 notes and therefore there was only a finite amount of music possible. At that point Brahms and Tchaikovsky had not yet been born nor jazz created. -Thomas Sowell

One of the best New Year's resolutions I ever made, some years ago, was to stop trying to reason with unreasonable people. -Thomas Sowell

It's ok to be ignorant; it's not ok to be stupid. –Dean Kalahar

High-tech communications of the 21st century are a force multiplier, in real time conveying the failures of redistributionist schemes... A nurse in Des Moines has ...more information than what the aristocratic class was privileged to obtain just a few decades ago. -Victor Davis Hanson

Human ingenuity, as it turns out, is the most precious resource. –Jonathan Last

Human imagination is the ultimate resource.- Julian Simon

When there is a void of information, you fill it with the worst case scenario. –unknown

Knowledge which is acquired under compulsion obtains no hold on the mind. –Plato

Every man is, no doubt, by nature, first and principally recommended to his own care; and as he is fitter to care of himself than of any other person, it is fit and right that it should be so. -Adam Smith

Distributed wisdom trumps individual knowledge. -Dean Kalahar

The "fatal conceit" - Friedrich Hayek

It is largely because civilization enables us constantly to profit from knowledge which we individually do not possess and because each individual's use of his particular knowledge may serve to assist others unknown to him in achieving their ends that men as members of civilized society can pursue their individual ends so much more successfully than they could alone. -F. A. Hayek

Following the kind of reasoning used by those who say it is futile to build more roads to cope with traffic congestion, it would be possible to say that it is "futile" to deal with hunger by eating because people just get hungry again later on. -Thomas Sowell

If knowledge is the scarcest resource, then ignorance would have to be the most common behavior. –Dean Kalahar

The reason life gets better is that ideas have sex. Ideas spread through trade, and when they meet they can mate, and you can produce combinations of different ideas. When this happens a lot, everyone gets smarter and the world gets better –John Stossel via Matt Ridley

If man is not to do more harm than good in his efforts to improve the social order, he will have to learn that in this, as in all other fields where essential complexity of an organized kind prevails, he cannot acquire the full knowledge which would make mastery of the events possible. He will therefore have to use what knowledge he can achieve, not to shape the results as the craftsman shapes his handiwork, but rather to cultivate a growth by providing the appropriate environment, in the manner which the gardener does this for his plants. –Friedrich Hayek

The recognition of the insuperable limits to his knowledge ought to indeed teach the student of society a lesson of humility which should guard him against becoming an accomplice in man's fatal striving to control society- a striving which makes him not only a tyrant over his fellows, but which may well make him the destroyer of a civilization which no brain has designed but which has grown from the free efforts of millions of individuals. –Friedrich Hayek

Laws

Laws are made for men of ordinary understanding and should, therefore, be construed by the ordinary rules of common sense. Their meaning is not to be sought for in metaphysical subtleties which may make anything mean everything or nothing at pleasure. -Thomas Jefferson

Why has government been instituted at all, because the passions of men will not conform to the dictates of reason and justice without constraint? -Alexander Hamilton

A government of laws and not of men -John Adams

The role of the government (in a free society)…is to do something that the market cannot do for itself, namely, to determine the rules of the game. -Milton Friedman

Laws do not represent reason. They represent force. -Walter E. Williams

If men were angels, no government would be necessary. If angels were to govern men, neither external nor internal controls on government would be necessary. -James Madison

There are two parts of good government, one is obedience of citizens to the laws, the other part is the goodness of the laws which they obey. -Aristotle

Law evolved as an expression of the natural feelings and experiences of human beings in general, not the articulated rationality of intellectual or moral leaders. -Thomas Sowell

The judge's moral duty is to faithfully carry out the law he was sworn to uphold, not sincerely change the law to produce better results as he sees them. -Thomas Sowell

We are either a nation of laws or a lawless nation.-Dean Kalahar

Any man or woman who robs any garden, public or private, while weeding it or who willfully pulls up any root vegetable, herb, or flower to spoil or waste or steal it, or robs any vineyard or gathers the grapes, or steals any ears of corn . . . shall be punished with death.
-Sir Thomas Dale

Leadership

Don't argue about who should have seen the iceberg when you should be getting people into lifeboats. –Thomas Sowell

British Prime Minister Margaret Thatcher gave the best definition of "consensus": Lack of leadership. -Thomas Sowell

Don't expect to build up the weak by pulling down the strong.
–Calvin Coolidge

Liberalism

At the heart of liberalism is the naïve belief that people are basically good. As a result of this belief, liberals rarely blame people for the evil they do. Instead, they blame economics, parents, capitalism, racism, and anything else that can let the individual off the hook. A second naïve liberal belief is that because people are basically good, talking with people who do evil is always better than fighting, let alone killing, them.
-Dennis Prager

Here's how it plays out with liberals; if you mention Christ on this side of the aisle they will bring up Darwin, if you then say 'ok I believe in

Darwin's survival of the fittest,' they will then say you should be more Christ like in your giving. -Dennis Miller

Leaders who sit in ivory towers or endless committee meetings have little contact with the knowledge of the people. Sadly, they are the first to proclaim they "feel your pain" and "understand your needs." This ironic condescension is an all too typical reaction from a group who deals in feelings instead of facts. -Dean Kalahar

Liberalism is totalitarianism with a human face. -Thomas Sowell

The same demigods who blame institutions for man's evil nature dismiss the fact that men, like themselves, created the institutions. -Dean Kalahar

The conceit of the anointed knows no bounds. -John Stossel

Moral rights in the unconstrained vision are rights to results. -Thomas Sowell

John Milton said, Better to reign in hell than serve in heaven. Liberals would sooner rule in hell than share in heaven. –Dean Kalahar

It is no wonder the left's causes take on a pseudo-religious faith in their certainty (i.e. global warming), and why they advance their beliefs from a purely emotional and ideological dogma. Their anger is misdirected fear that their worldview might come crashing down, like a house of cards, if heaven forbid anything indeed challenged their "reality." It affirms a life of identity confusion being played out as self-assuredness. –Dean Kalahar

Liberals have more questions than answers; conservatives have more answers than questions. -Anonymous

For the anointed, it is desperately important to win, not simply because they believe that one policy or set of beliefs and values is better for society, but because their whole sense of themselves is at stake. -Thomas Sowell

Everyone is a "progressive" by his own lights. That the anointed believe that this label differentiates themselves from other people is one of a number of symptoms of their naïve narcissism. -Thomas Sowell

Liberals hold evolutionary theory as a cornerstone of reason and yet feel the need to ignore its principles and supplant natural law with man as the social engineer? -Dean Kalahar

Liberals feel terrible about their own exclusivity and the abyss between what is professed and what is lived, an angst over their voluntary segregation that is ameliorated by loudly and cheaply alleging that someone else is racist. –Victor Davis Hanson

The vision of the anointed is one in which such ills as poverty, irresponsible sex, and crime derive primarily from "society," rather than from individual choices and behavior. To believe in personal responsibility would be to destroy the whole special role of the anointed, whose vision casts them in the role of rescuers of people treated unfairly by "society." -Thomas Sowell

The champions of socialism call themselves progressives, but they recommend a system which is characterized by rigid observance of routine and by a resistance to every kind of improvement. They call themselves liberals, but they are intent upon abolishing liberty. They call themselves democrats, but they yearn for dictatorship. They call themselves revolutionaries, but they want to make the government omnipotent. -Ludwig von Mises

[To liberals] our mastery of nature must extend to human nature as well. A society that can call anywhere in the world on a cell phone, must just as easily end war, poverty, or unhappiness, as if these pathologies are strictly materially caused, not impoverishments of the soul.
-Victor Davis Hansen

The evident panic of the progressive mind stems from a paradox as old as progressivism in America. Progressives see themselves as the only legitimate representatives of ordinary people. Yet their vision of what democracy requires frequently conflicts with what majorities believe and how they choose to live. Add to this the progressive belief that human beings can be perfected through the rule of experts, and you have a recipe—when the people make choices contrary to progressive dictates—for generating contempt among the experts for the people whose interests they claim to alone represent...The progressive mind is on a collision course with itself. The clash between its democratic pretensions and its authoritarian predilections. -Peter Berkowitz

There's an infuriating tendency among mainstream liberal historians to take two approaches to evils in American history. Sins are always either the result of conservatives doing conservative things or they're the product of America's fundamentally bigoted nature. It's just never, ever, the case that liberalism or progressivism has something to apologize for. Liberalism is never wrong, because essential to the concept of liberalism is the idea that it must always be right. The fact that racism and other evils were commonplace, even central, to much of the progressive project is simply too jarring to contemplate and so we get either a whitewash or blame-shifting. –Jonah Goldberg

In his devotion to the pursuit of happiness, modern man has forgotten how to suffer. The dream of a painless world is the great illusion of liberalism. Classical liberalism, it is true, never promised to make men happier; it promised only to make them richer. Adam Smith argued that we deceive ourselves when we suppose that those material luxuries that we associate with happiness are "worth all the toil and anxiety which we are so apt to bestow" on their attainment.

Material wealth is good, Smith says, not because it makes us permanently happier, but because it enables us to dispense, in some measure, with physical and corporeal miseries (hunger, squalor, disease, and the like...

Smith's classical liberalism has all but entirely given way to a modern liberalism which regards suffering not as something inherent in the very nature of life but as an anomaly to be eradicated by reason and science and social legislation...

The "pain which is essential to life cannot be thrown off," Schopenhauer says. "The ceaseless efforts to banish suffering accomplish no more than to make it change its form..."

Delusory though it is, liberalism's dream of an anodyne world persists because it appeals to our inner egotism and self-conceit. When something painful happens to one, one's instinct is to be outraged, as though the universe had made a mistake in abrogating one's right to an ideal and perfect felicity. But there has been no mistake; we have been created to know joy, and also to know misery. -Michael Knox Beran

Liberals are the aggressors in the culture war (and not always for the worse, as the civil-rights movement demonstrates). What they object to isn't so much the government imposing its values on people — heck, they love that. They see nothing wrong with imposing their views about diet, exercise, sex, race, and the environment on Americans. What outrages them is resistance or even non-compliance with their agenda. "Why are you making such a scene?" progressives complain. "Just do what we want, and there will be no fuss"...-You're either with us, or against us — which means we shall be against you. -Jonah Goldberg

The Soviet Union, Cuba, Vietnam, and North Korea are all examples of oppressive failures based on wealth redistribution. How can modern liberals embrace the tyrannical system that robs incentive and dooms an entire society to a mediocre standard of living dictated by central planning? When will liberals learn that the utopia they seek is right under their feet. All they need to do is quit trying to cultivate it and let it grow on its own. – Glen Risley

When the voices of the Left all come together, the amplification is stupefying. The result is that a morally bankrupt, politically tyrannical, economically destructive party is able to set the course of an entire nation and put it on the road to disaster...

"Progressive," "socialist," and "liberal" are interchangeable terms that describe members of a moral crusade. The goal of the crusade is "social justice," or its equivalent: *equality*. The quest for this utopia of social and economic equality is what forges their alliances, defines their allegiances, and justifies the means they use to get there. They may differ on particular policies and tactics to advance the cause, but if they are Democrats or supporters of the Democrats, they see the party as the practical vehicle for making the idea a reality...

To transform society, you need the power of the state; it is the only way their future can be achieved. That is why they are willing to follow the marching orders of a party that can control the state, and that is why they want to advance its fortunes. The Democrats' perennial campaign message — Republicans are conducting a war on minorities, women, working Americans, and the poor — rests on the central idea that unites progressives behind the party: *We are for equality, they are against it...*

If the cause is about changing the world and there is only one party that can acquire the means to do it, then even though it may be wrong on this or that matter, its fortunes must be advanced and its power defended. This commitment is magnified when the opposition party is viewed as the enemy of the noble cause. If Republicans are seen as the party of privilege at war with minorities, women, and the poor, then their ideas are not only wrong but evil...

Because Democrats and progressives regard politics as a battle of good versus evil, their focus is not on policies that work and ideas that make sense, but on what will make their party win. Demonizing the opposition is one answer; unity is another. If we are divided, we will fail, and that means evil will triumph...

The issues are never the issues; the issue is always what will bring power to those who are on the right side of history, because their cause — not any particular policy or tactic — is enlightened and just. This intoxicating belief is the key not only to the power of the party but to the sense of individual achievement and self-worth of its members, as soldiers in a moral cause...

Here is the bottom line: If conservatives continue to ignore the fact that their opponents approach politics as a religious war, if they fail to organize their own resistance as a moral cause, they will eventually lose the war and everything that depends on it... -David Horowitz

Arrogant groupthink not only leads to bad policies, but it also reinforces a mass psychology that simply takes it for granted that liberals have sole access to the Truth. It's like having God on your side without having to believe in God... the liberal tribe seems to champion such freedoms only when they line up with its own worldview. You can have all the freedom and autonomy you want, so long as it yields progressive ends. But if you don't want to bake a wedding cake for a gay wedding, or if you're a nun who doesn't want to pay for something you don't need and are morally opposed to, that's too bad. The right to be wrong, in liberals' eyes, is a right only liberals should have. –Jonah Goldberg

Liberal ideology so often proves more important than people. Noble theories about saving humanity offer exemption from worry about the immediate consequences for individual humans. In a personal sense, those who embrace progressive ideas expect to be excused from the ramifications of their schemes. –Victor Davis Hanson

5 arguments of simple minds and liberal politicians:
1. The "straw man" argument– They say something was said that no one would say.
2. The "it's settled" argument – Saying "there are no other arguments."
3. The "it's working, everything is fine" argument. Leave it be.
4. The "all disagreement is a dishonorable attack" argument.
5. The "poetic truth" argument – State what sounds perfectly obvious as a form of moral intimidation, not reason,
-Dean Kalahar via George Will & Shelby Steele,

Liberal exemplification

The psychological defense mechanism for liberals is exemplification: self-righteousness and pseudo-moral authority. –Dean Kalahar

Liberal privilege

Unmentioned is the strange phenomenon of de facto white affirmative action — the old-boy/old-girl network of New York and Washington elites, who get their kids into Sidwell Friends or Exeter as boot camp for Yale or Princeton, either by an opportune phone call or by the sort of lifelong neurotic prepping that only contacts and money can provide. That results in the spectacle of the nearly all-white New Republic seeking absolution for its apartheid by publishing an article on Republicans' supposed lack of interest in minorities.
-Victor Davis Hanson

Liberty

They that can give up essential liberty to obtain a little temporary safety deserve neither liberty nor safety. -Benjamin Franklin

God grants liberty only to those who love it, and are always ready to guard and defend it. -Daniel Webster

Is life so dear or peace so sweet as to be purchased at the price of chains and slavery? Forbid it, Almighty God! I know not what course others may take, but as for me, give me liberty or give me death! -Patrick Henry

The tree of liberty must be refreshed from time to time with the blood of patriots and tyrants. -Thomas Jefferson

Life, liberty, and property do not exist because men have made laws. On the contrary, it was the fact that life, liberty, and property existed beforehand that caused men to make laws in the first place. -Frederic Bastiat

Forced health kills liberty. -Dean Kalahar

If there were omniscient men, if we could know not only all that affects the attainment of our present wishes but also our future wants and desires, there would be little case for liberty. And, in turn, liberty of the individual would, of course, make complete foresight impossible. Liberty is essential in order to leave room for the unforeseeable and unpredictable; we want it because we have learned to expect from it the opportunity of realizing many of our aims. It is because every individual knows so little and, in particular, because we rarely know which of us knows best that we trust the independent and competitive efforts of many to induce the emergence of what we shall want when we see it. -F.A. Hayek

It is the duty of the patriot to protect his country from his government. -Thomas Paine

'Emergencies' have always been the pretext on which the safeguards of individual liberty have been eroded. –Friedrich Von Hayek

We must all hang together, or, assuredly, we shall all hang separately -Benjamin Franklin

Because the moral superiority of liberty is irrefutable, totalitarians often feel the need to wrap barbarism in the language of freedom. –Jonah Goldberg

In Europe, charters of liberty have been granted by power, but America has charters of power granted by liberty. –James Madison

Life

Three main questions of life: Who am I, Will someone love who I am? Will someone recognize my accomplishments – Erickson, Spinoza, Kalahar

It's the Serengeti plain, if someone is going to perpetually exhibit a limp they are going to get feed on, that's the vigorish of life and they are going to have to buck up to that bar, that's the way life works.
-Dennis Miller

There is no perfection. Even the earth is tilted. -Dean Kalahar

I have a lot of growing up to do. I realized that the other day in my fort.
-Zach Galifinakis

Once you realize life is hard it becomes easier.-Unknown

The vast majority of people in the world right now can only dream of being in your shoes. -Dean Kalahar

It takes some time to wear out the tires on the road to understanding life.
-Dean Kalahar

Each man makes his own happiness and is responsible for his own problems. -Roy A, Kroc

Life becomes easier when you learn to accept an apology you never got.
-Anonymous

Don't take life so seriously, it's not like you're going to get out alive.
-Anonymous

All the art of living lies in a firm mingling of letting go and holding on.
–Henry Ellis

Limited government

My reading of history convinces me that most bad government has grown out of too much government.-Thomas Jefferson
The powers delegated by the proposed Constitution to the federal government are few and defined. Those which are to remain in the State government are numerous and indefinite. -James Madison

Man is not free unless government is limited. There is a clear cause and effect her that is as neat and predictable as a law of physics; as government expands, liberty contracts. -Ronald Reagan

Government exists to protect us from each other. Where government has gone beyond its limits is in deciding to protect us from ourselves. -Ronald Reagan

Many people want their government to protect the consumer. A much more urgent problem is to protect the consumer from the government. -Milton Friedman

Love

God, let me live just one hour longer than him: let me be there for him in all ways for 'always." –Mary M. Glaser's mothers prayer

Loyalty

Loyalty can be a virtue, but it is a secondary virtue when it conflicts with principles and a vice when it's only a function of ambition. –Bret Stephens

Luck

I find that the harder I work, the more luck I seem to have. -Thomas Jefferson

Malcontents

Malcontents are perennially unhappy because what they castigate has given them everything they treasure, and they are either too weak or too human to confess it. -Victor Davis Hanson

Marriage

In the 1970s, 73 percent of adults with a high-school degree or some college were in intact first marriages. In the 2000s, 45 percent were. In the 1970s, 50 percent of blacks at that level of education were in intact first marriages. In the 2000s, 33 percent were. As recently as 1982, just 13 percent of births to people with this level of education were out-of-wedlock. In the late 2000s, 44 percent were. Among blacks with a high-school degree or some college, the figure was 75 percent. Males with a high-school education have been dropping out of the labor force for decades. One flip side is a drastic increase in the rolls of Social Security Disability Insurance, despite better medical care and less-strenuous jobs. -Rich Lowry

No one quite knows what the advent of gay marriage will entail, once the idea of marriage as the exclusivity of a single man, joined with a single woman, to promote procreation has ended. But the theoretical possibilities of bold new unions, both sincere and cynical, are now as endless as they are taboo to discuss publicly. –Victor Davis Hanson

"It's not about expanding marriage, it's about destroying marriage." That would be the most obvious explanation as to why the same societal groups who assured us in the Seventies that marriage was either (a) a "meaningless piece of paper" or (b) institutionalized rape are now insisting it's a universal human right. They've figured out what, say, terrorist-turned-educator Bill Ayers did — that, when it comes to destroying core civilizational institutions, trying to blow them up is less effective than hollowing them out from within. -Mark Stein

According to a fascinating Harvard study on the subject, is the prevalence of marriage in their communities. It matters whether a poor child has married parents, that is, but it matters even more how many of his friends and classmates have married parents. –Kevin Williamson

Means & ends

Means and ends must cohere because the end is pre-existent in the means, and ultimately destructive means cannot bring about constructive ends. -Dr. Martin Luther King Jr.

Means (method & incentives created) are just as important as the ends (goals). Only looking at the ends while ignoring the means disregards the behavioral component of motivation and self-interest and thus creates a situation where failure is almost guaranteed. -Dean Kalahar

In the age of liberal indulgence and exemption ... noble ends sometimes must justify tawdry means. -Victor Davis Hansen

If we talk a good game to the public we ought to play a good game for the public. - Dean Kalahar

Medicine

I'm telling you that the cure is the disease. The main source of illness in this world is the doctor's own illness: his compulsion to try and cure and his fraudulent belief that he can. It ain't easy to do nothing.
-Samuel Shem

Minimum wage

What minimum wage laws do is lower the cost of, and hence subsidize, racial preference indulgence. After all, if an employer must pay the same wage no matter whom he hires, the cost of discriminating in favor of the people he prefers is cheaper. -Walter Williams

Although packaged as compassionate legislation helping the poor and downtrodden members of society, the minimum wage allows employers a legal way to discriminate. -Dean Kalahar

I've found that the minimum wage issue is a pretty accurate litmus test for basic economic literacy. Defenders of government price controls like the minimum wage really can't be taken seriously because they haven't yet mastered basic economic principles and don't yet understand the fundamental laws of supply and demand. -Mark Perry

In the U.S., the Davis-Bacon Act of 1931 (still on the books), a super minimum wage law, was enacted to protect unionized white construction workers from competition with black workers. The support ran along the lines of Alabama (Democrat) Rep. Clayton Allgood's testimony: "That contractor has cheap colored labor that he transports, and he puts them in cabins, and it is labor of that sort that is in competition with white labor throughout the country." (Congressional Record, 1931, page 6513). What minimum wage laws do is lower the cost of, and hence subsidize, racial preference indulgence. After all, if an employer must pay the same wage no matter whom he hires, the cost of discriminating in favor of the people he prefers is cheaper. -Walter Williams

Modern Men

Many modern American men,.. don't know how to do anything manly anymore. And by "manly," I do not mean "physical." A lot of us do physical things, but these are yuppie fitness things like "spinning," and "crunches," and working on our "core," and running half-marathons and then putting "13.1" stickers on our hybrid cars so everybody will know what total cardiovascular badasses we are…That's not manly. I'll tell you who was manly: The early American pioneers. They set out into the vast untracked wilderness with nothing but a musket and a sack of hardtack and hominy, and they had to survive out there for months, even years, completely on their own, sleeping on the ground in bear-infested forests… the point is, these pioneering men did not do "crunches." These men crunched the damn continent—blazing trails, fording rivers, crossing mountain ranges, building log cabins, forging things with forges, etc. We modern men can't do any of those things. We don't have the vaguest idea how to ford a river. We'd check our phones to see if we had a fording app and, if not, we'd give up, go back home and work on our cores. -Dave Berry

Monopoly

In short, loose use of the word "monopoly," in a political sense quite different from its economic meaning, often leads to policies reducing competition and thus producing the very monopolistic results so loudly denounced. -Thomas Sowell

There's no conspiracy here of big oil or big auto. It's a conspiracy of physics. -Robert Bryce

Morality

The first principle of a free society is that each person owns himself ... Once one accepts the principle of self-ownership, what's moral and immoral becomes self-evident. Murder is immoral because it violates private property. Rape and theft are also immoral; they also violate private property. -Walter Williams

Today in the western world there is no general acknowledgement of an external standard or reference for how man should conduct himself. The thoughts that guided the old Western thought have been replaced with secular political and scientific utopias instead of a religious expectation of a salvation located outside of time and history. The current belief is that man is eugenic or can improve his genetic hereditary makeup by a nihilistic practice of changing the existing political and social institutions. By this new view of the world, man is autonomous and has absolute freedom to do whatever he chooses without regard to universal truths or the or the old Western belief that there are moral laws and rights that transcend man and his behavior. -William Pfaff

The west no longer acknowledges the existence of an external rule-giver or moral authority. It regards mankind as entirely autonomous, existing within a moral framework entirely of its own creation, with responsibility only to self. -William Pfaff

Morality can't be legislated, but behavior can be regulated. Judicial decrees may not change the heart, but they can restrain the heartless. -Dr. Martin Luther King Jr.

It is a mark of the moral illiteracy of our times that it even has to be argued that suffering the indignity of having a baker refuse to service your wedding because he holds ideas about marriage that were shared by, among others, Barack Obama until the day before yesterday, may be painful, even humiliating, but it is an experience that is not very much like being a member of a captive race that was held in slavery for centuries and then systematically subjugated for another century...

Try turning the moral math around as a thought experiment: Imagine you are the gay owner of a restaurant in Chelsea, a member in good standing of the National Gay and Lesbian Chamber of Commerce, rainbow flag flying out front — and the cretins from the Westboro Baptist Church decide that they want to rent your party room for their annual "God Hates Fags" Sunday brunch. Shouldn't you have the right to refuse? There is in this sad world such a thing as a Ku Klux Klan wedding — should the management of Harlem's famous Sylvia's Restaurant be prosecuted under civil-rights law if the establishment should decline to cater such a wedding? It is impossible for me to imagine that that should be the case... "Live and let live" implies a two-way relationship.-Kevin Williamson

Nature

Going green, or back to nature, is going back to barbarism, poverty, ignorance, and human suffering. -Dean Kalahar

For humans, living in "nature" meant a short life span marked by violence, disease and ignorance. People who work for the end of poverty and relief from disease are fighting against nature. -Ross McKitrick

Nothing in the world is more flexible and yielding than water. Yet when it attacks the firm and the strong, none can withstand it. -Lao-Tzu

Natural ingredients

When some advertiser says that its product is "made from natural ingredients," just what does that mean? Since businesses do not create matter out of nothing, but simply transform the matter that already exists, everything is made from natural ingredients. -Thomas Sowell

Negotiation

Negotiations are not a substitute for force. When international negotiations work, often it is because aggressors know what is going to happen if it doesn't work. -Thomas Sowell

Negotiation is not a policy. It is a technique. It is a way of achieving our objectives. It doesn't tell us what the objectives are. -John Bolton

Non-judgmental

How anyone can argue in favor of being non-judgmental is beyond me. To say that being non-judgmental is better than being judgmental is itself a judgment, and therefore a violation of the principle. -Thomas Sowell

Oppressed (the)

The contemporary leftist theory that groups certified as "oppressed" deserve special treatment at the expense of the "privileged." Such a view, however, collapses in its own illogic. A system that gives special treatment to members of an "oppressed" group is simply a new variety of privilege. –James Taranto

The Cuban government's brutal food-denial program is not a benevolent attempt to fight obesity, save the environment, or demonstrate the wonders of organic farming. It, like Stalin's Holodomor, the Nazis' "Hunger Plan" for the territories they occupied during the war, and the current North Korean regime's enforced starvation policy, is an effort to destroy the will of a population to resist tyranny through denial of the most essential substances necessary to maintain life and strength. The use of hunger as a weapon of political control is a crime against humanity. –Robert Zubrin

Order/disorder

Order is not the order that is imposed by society, by a culture, by environment, by compulsion or obedience. Order is not a blueprint; it comes into being when you understand disorder, not only outside you but in yourself. Through the negation of disorder is order. Therefore we must look at the disorder of our life, the contradictions in ourselves, the opposing desires, saying one thing and doing, thinking another. -Jiddu Krishnamurti

Panacea

Nothing is a panacea — or else, by definition, all the problems of the world would already be solved. -Thomas Sowell

Peace

[The idea that]Peace is always possible, no matter the circumstances—comes from the Christmas Day Truce of 1914. It is the story of two regiments—one British, the other German—that celebrated Christmas during World War I by playing soccer in No Man's Land. For the antagonists mired in the freezing mud of Ypres, their vision of Christmas yet-to-come was bleak indeed. Nevertheless, late on Christmas Eve, a German regiment gathered to sing "Stille Nacht, Heilige Nacht." British troops responded from their side by singing the English version, and soon the night air was filled with the rich harmony of the men's voices. In the morning came a tentative wave, followed by an exchange of messages and then the first handshake. It was the British who produced the ball, and the Germans who won the match, 3-2. –Amanda Foreman

Perception

We judge motion by acceleration, or a change in velocity; so to make a judgment of reason, one must change cognitive speed by shifting the way one is thinking. -Dean Kalahar via Dan Niel.

All modern social science deals with perceptions, but that is a misnomer because it neglects to distinguish between perceptions and misperceptions. – Harvey Mansfield

Perspective

When you get up in the morning and feed your dog he looks up at you and thinks: "She comes, finds my food and pours it for me—she must be a god." A cat thinks: "She comes, finds my food and pours it out for me—I must be a god." –Friend of Peggy Noonan

Fish don't know he's wet. –Funkadellic

When I was growing up I didn't want to be President, I wanted to be Willie Mays. –George W. Bush

If you judge a fish by its ability to climb a tree, it will live its whole life believing that it is stupid. – Unknown, but it was not Albert Einstein

Planning

Everyone has a plan until you punch them in the face. Then they don't have a plan anymore. – Mike Tyson

Failing to plan is planning to fail. -Winston Churchill

A goal without a plan is just a wish. -Antoine de Saint-Exupery

Platitudes

A good way to test if someone is speaking in platitudes is to ask yourself if you can imagine a normal human adult believing the opposite...Consider today's fashionable calls for "sustainability."
–Donald Boudreux

Poetic truth

Like poetic license ("poetic truth") bends the actual truth in order to put forward a larger and more essential truth—one that, of course, serves one's cause. Poetic truths succeed by casting themselves as perfectly obvious: "America is a racist nation"; "the immigration debate is driven by racism"... And we say, "Yes, of course," lest we seem to be racist. Poetic truths work by moral intimidation, not reason.
–Shelby Steele, The decline of the Civil Rights Establishment

Political accountability

(If people act up out of ideology) You ask for an apology, not for the beliefs but for the behavior. If you want to have people behave respectfully, you don't reward those who behave badly. -Bruce Slinguff

Political correctness

Moral relativity/equivalency, multiculturalism, tolerance, secular humanism and a host of other political correct du jour's bring on rather than avoid conflict and killing, and breed rather than eradicate ignorance and violence, so they are not ethical ideas but instead are anti-rational and amoral in every sense of the word. -Dean Kalahar via V.D. Hansen

Of all the economic delusions maybe the most dangerous is political correctness (PC). The idea that what sounds politically and socially palatable must be the best solution to a problem is thinly veiled intellectual thought. -Dean Kalahar

Political correctness is a position based solely on what sounds good and feels right. -Dean Kalahar

What we are experiencing is terrorism of the politically correct variety. A cultural war is being raged in America by a progressive "tolerance" movement that is intolerant toward many institutional traditions, principles, and laws that were created and tested over thousands of years of trial and error. The attackers show a condescending hypocrisy of moral relativism towards any concept that might interfere with their self-anointed sensibilities of creating a utopia so as to avoid self awareness. -Dean Kalahar

More children die each year from bicycle accidents than from gun accidents, but where is there any such orchestrated hysteria about a need to ban bicycles? -Thomas Sowell

Are we being bullied into believing bullying is bad? -Dean Kalahar

Conventional morality, secular humanism, moral relativity, or moral equivalencies are all similar principles that guide modern political correctness. These visions ignore basic principles of scarcity and cost leading to policies that are more concerned with doing what feels right than what is correct based on sound economic principles. -Dean Kalahar

The PC crowd sees the world and its workings from the realm of what they feel is common sense and what they have been told is conventional wisdom. As such, their analysis of problems and possible solutions only look to what can be seen in the here and now. Unfortunately, what sounds right or correct is often, as we have seen, the exact wrong thing to do in terms of economics. Because feelings and an emotional divining rod is substituted for empirical evidence and analysis, most people are easily swayed by inaccurate economic arguments. -Dean Kalahar

The good news is that the market can handle and disseminate PC ideas that are inefficient. The bad news is that those who do not want their values judged in economic terms with costs and benefits factored in must look to other arenas. To counteract market forces, do-gooders who need to feel well of themselves push their PC agenda through the government institution instead of the free market because their ideas would never have a chance of gaining traction anywhere else. They add insult to injury by using taxpayers' dollars to pay for their emotional fads.
-Dean Kalahar

Politics

In every crisis, Washington suffers from a predictable case of "do something" disease. -Jonathan Williams

A government that robs Peter to pay Paul can always depend on the support of Paul. -George Bernard Shaw

Demagoguery is the last refuge of the spineless politician willing to do anything to win the next election. -Marco Rubio

When you see a four-year-old bossing a two-year-old, you are seeing the fundamental problem of the human race—and the reason so many idealistic political movements for a better world have ended in mass-murdering dictatorships. Giving leaders enough power to create "social justice" is giving them enough power to destroy all justice, all freedom, and all human dignity.-Thomas Sowell

Turning the empirical question of the results of policy A versus the results of policy B into the more personal question of a wonderful Us versus a terrible Them makes it harder to retreat if the facts do not bear out the belief.-Thomas Sowell

When utopian ideas take hold over a group of individuals, an ideology is born. This in and of itself is not a problem, but ideologies have the ability to turn into socio-political movements that can be dangerous.
-Dean Kalahar

Nothing is worse that an elite that demands egalitarianism for others but ensures privilege for itself. -Victor Davis Hansen

Any politician can promise a new project, an expanded entitlement or a special-interest tax break with someone else's money, but only a statesman can explain exactly how it is all to be paid for.
-Victor Davis Hanson

Unfortunately, people on the make seem to have a keener appreciation of the power of words, as the magic road to other power, than do people defending values that seem to them too obvious to require words.
-Thomas Sowell

You can only aim for equality by giving some people the right to take things from others. And what ultimately happens when you aim for equality is that A and B decide what C should do for D. Except that they take a little bit of commission off on the way. - Milton Friedman

Politics like magic creates "the unwilling suspension of disbelief." Economics like gravity destroys the willing belief in utopia."
-Dean Kalahar via Penn Gillette

Politicians invariably respond to crises -- that in most cases they themselves created -- by spawning new government programs, laws and regulations. These, in turn, generate more havoc and poverty, which inspires the politicians to create more programs . . . and the downward spiral repeats itself until the productive sectors of the economy collapse under the collective weight of taxes and other burdens imposed in the name of fairness, equality and do-goodism." -Steven Moore

Enforced egalitarianism entails the death of excellence. For it seizes the rewards that excellence earns and turns them over to politicians and bureaucrats for distribution to the mediocrities upon whose votes they depend. -Patrick Buchanan

When sound bites generate a disingenuous picture that is easy for the public to digest, the roots of the PC problem take hold. –Dean Kalahar

The welfare state is the oldest con game in the world. First you take the people's money quietly and then you give some of it back to them flamboyantly. -Thomas Sowell

If political conflicts are reduced to contests between the wimps and the barbarians, the barbarians are going to win -Thomas Sowell

The whole aim of practical politics is to keep the populace alarmed (and hence clamorous to be led to safety) by menacing it with an endless series of hobgoblins, all of them imaginary. -H.L. Mencken

When people want the impossible, only liars can satisfy them. -Thomas Sowell

A politician who is poor is a poor politician. -Carlos Hank Gonzalez

Spending is oxygen to politicians, and growing revenues represent a gusher of fresh air. –John Tamny

The art of politics consists in looking only at the immediate effects of any act or policy; it consists in tracing the consequences of that policy only for a favored special interest group while ignoring the consequences of that policy on all other groups and the community as a whole. -Mark Perry via Henry Hazlitt

Population

In reality, the entire population of the world today could be housed in the state of Texas, in a single-story, single-family houses-four to a house-and with a typical yard around each home. -Thomas Sowell

Post-modernism

Postmodernist is a trendy word for someone who leaves academia believing that there are not really absolute facts, but merely competing ideas and discourses. In this view, particular ideologies unfortunately gain credibility as establishment icons only from the relative advantage that arises from race, class, and gender biases. -Victor Davis Hanson

Poverty

Hard as it may appear in individual instances, dependent poverty ought to be held disgraceful. Such a stimulus seems to be absolutely necessary to promote the happiness to the great masses of mankind, and every general attempt to weaken this stimulus, however benevolent its apparent intention, will always defeat its own purpose. -Thomas Robert Malthus

The problem in poor countries is that people do not have ownership (a recording system of titles, deeds, formal property records, etc.) over their land and possessions because the rights to these possessions are not documented under a system of law...Without a system of formal legal ownership, the incentive for acting on resources to create additional wealth is fruitless. In order to foster capitalism, a nation must have in place a stable government institution that includes constitutional law, order, justice and property rights. -Dean Kalahar via Hernando DeSoto

People in developing countries do not live with specific institutions operating within the framework of life, liberty and property that allow for wealth creation through the development of resources. -Dean Kalahar via Hernando DeSoto

If you could solve only one social ill—either inequality or poverty—which would it be? Or suppose that the only way to address poverty would be to allow inequality: Would you allow it? This seems a no-brainer: poverty is a far larger factor in human misery than is inequality. If we could have steadily fewer people suffering from grinding poverty, is that not something to wish for, even if it comes with inequality? This appears to be the position in which we find ourselves. The only way we have discovered to raise people out of poverty is the institutions of capitalism, and those institutions allow inequality. Keeping people in poverty seems too high a price to pay in the service of equality. One is tempted to say that only a person who has never experienced poverty could think differently. -James Otteson

The question is how can we as people exercise our responsibility toward our fellow man most effectively. So far as poverty is concerned, there has never in history been a more effective machine for eliminating poverty than the free enterprise system and the free market."
-Milton Friedman

We have spent $15 trillion "fighting" poverty since 1965 and we are currently spending $ 1 trillion a year — an amount equal to about $22,000 per poor person or $88,000 for a family of four. Yet our poverty rate today (16%) is higher than when we started (14%)! If there has been a War on Poverty, poverty won. Is it not obvious that we are subsidizing and enabling a way of life? To put it bluntly, we are paying young women to have children out of wedlock. We are paying them to be unemployed. And we are paying them to remain poor. –John Goodman

If the opposite of poverty is wealth
And if wealth is best created by capitalism
Then the solution to poverty is capitalism. –Dean Kalahar

The Census Bureau pegs the poverty rate among blacks at 35 percent and among whites at 13 percent. The illegitimacy rate among blacks is 72 percent, and among whites it's 30 percent. A statistic that one doesn't hear much about is that the poverty rate among black married families has been in the single digits for more than two decades, currently at 8 percent. For married white families, it's 5 percent. Now the politically incorrect questions: Whose fault is it to have children without the benefit of marriage and risk a life of dependency? Do people have free will, or are they governed by instincts? -Walter Williams

There may be some pinhead sociologists who blame the weak black family structure on racial discrimination. But why was the black illegitimacy rate only 14 percent in 1940? –Walter Williams

No one can blame a person if he starts out in life poor, because how one starts out is not his fault. If he stays poor, he is to blame because it is his fault. Avoiding long-term poverty is not rocket science. First, graduate from high school. Second, get married before you have children, and stay married. Third, work at any kind of job, even one that starts out paying the minimum wage. And finally, avoid engaging in criminal behavior. It turns out that a married couple, each earning the minimum wage, would earn an annual combined income of $30,000. The Census Bureau poverty line for a family of two is $15,500, and for a family of four, it's $23,000. By the way, no adult who starts out earning the minimum wage does so for very long. -Walter Williams

Far from having the 21st-century equivalent of an Edwardian class system, the United States is characterized by a great deal of variation in income: More than half of all adult Americans will be at or near the poverty line at some point over the course of their lives; 73 percent will also find themselves in the top 20 percent, and 39 percent will make it into the top 5 percent for at least one year. Perhaps most remarkable, 12 percent of Americans will be in the top 1 percent for at least one year of their working lives... the turnover among the super-rich (the top 400 taxpayers in any given year) is 98 percent over a decade — that is, just 2 percent of that elusive group remain there for ten years in a row. Among those earning more than $1 million a year, most earned that much for only one year of the nine-year period studied, and only 6 percent earned that much for the entire period. -Kevin Williamson via Mark R. Rank; Chasing the American Dream: Understanding What Shapes Our Fortunes

What is hereditary in the United States is not wealth but poverty.
-Kevin Williamson via Mark R. Rank

Power

Power tends to corrupt and absolute power corrupts absolutely.
-Lord Acton

Every man invested with power is apt to abuse it...to prevent this abuse, it is necessary from the very nature of things that power should be a check to power. -Montesquieu

Concentrated power is not rendered harmless by the good intentions of those who create it. The power to do good is also the power to do harm.
-Milton Friedman

The arts of power and its minions are the same in all countries and in all ages. It marks its victim; denounces it; and excites the public odium and the public hatred, to conceal its own abuses and encroachments.
-Henry Clay

Nothing has been more common in history than for victims to become oppressors when they gain power. -Thomas Sowell

The balance of power is the scale of peace. -Thomas Paine

All power is given
The more power you give, the more you get
Power is taken away from those who think they have it. -Dean Kalahar

Referent behaviors are attractive and are given power.

Intelligence	
Values	
Character =	Do what's right even if nobody is looking
Personality =	Genuine = possessing the claimed character, authentic, real, true, unaffected, open, honest, forthright.
Charming =	Pleasing, delightful, magical, lovely, winning, engaging
Charismatic =	A spiritual or personal quality that gives an individual influence, charm, magnetism, presence.
Respect	
Consistency	-Dean Kalahar

Power always thinks it has a great soul and vast views beyond the comprehension of the weak; and that it is doing God's service, when it is violating all His laws."-John Adams in a letter to Thomas Jefferson

Subtlety commands power. -Dean Kalahar

Giving money and power to government is like giving whiskey and car keys to teenage boys. -P.J. O'Rourke

Prices

Prices convert economic principles into actions. -Dean Kalahar

Price controls

The black market was a way of getting around government controls. It was a way of enabling the free market to work. It was a way of opening up, enabling people. -Milton Friedman

Shortages in health care will be brought about by the very government who promised to increase efficiencies in health care, which will cause unnecessary deaths. In short, government run health care will potentially kill you. –Dean Kalahar

Misconceptions about the economic function of prices lead not only to price controls, with all their counterproductive consequences, but also to organized attempts by various institutions, laws and policies to get those prices paid by somebody else. For society as a whole, there is no somebody else. Yet few of those in politics seem prepared to face the fact. Economists may say that there is no such thing as a free lunch but politicians get elected by promising free lunches. -Thomas Sowell

Principles

Names change, organizations change, allegiances change, principles do not. -Dean Kalahar

A people that values its privileges above its principles soon loses both. -Dwight Eisenhower

You can't personify principles. –Dean Kalahar

Private Property

The moment the idea is admitted into society, that property is not as sacred as the laws of God, and that there is not a force of law and public justice to protect it, anarchy and tyranny commence. -John Adams

Private property connects effort to reward. -John Stossel

The first principle of a free society is that each person owns himself. You are your private property and I am mine. -Walter Williams

Wherever there is great property, there is great inequality. For one very rich man there must be at least five hundred poor, and the affluence of the few supposes the indigence of the many. The affluence of the rich excites the indignation of the poor, who are often both driven by want, and prompted by envy, to invade his possessions. It is only under the shelter of the civil magistrate that the owner of that valuable property, which is acquired by the labor of many years, or perhaps of many successive generations, can sleep a single night in security. -Adam Smith

[A]s a man is said to have a right to his property, he may be equally said to have a property in his rights. -James Madison

Property is the fruit of labor-property is desirable - it is a positive good in the world. That some should be rich, shows that others may become rich, and hence is just encouragement to industry and enterprise. Let not who is houseless pull down the house of another; but let him labor diligently and build one for himself, thus by example assuring that his own shall be safe from violence. -Abraham Lincoln

John Locke, an intellectual source of American freedom, said that property rights, which he defined to include rights to "lives, liberties and estates," exist prior to, and independent of, government, and their preservation is "the great and chief end" for which governments are founded. Property rights provide a sphere of personal sovereignty, a zone of privacy into which government should be able to intrude only with difficulty and only so far. Because they are the basis of individual independence, America's Founders considered property rights the foundation of all other liberties, including self-government — the governance of one's self. –George Will

Nobody spends somebody else's money as carefully as he spends his own. Nobody uses somebody else's resources as carefully as he uses his own. So if you want efficiency and effectiveness, if you want knowledge to be properly utilized, you have to do it through the means of private property. -Milton Friedman

To prove the power of property rights in conservation of resources, place a bowl of candy in a room with a "please share" sign attached. -Dean Kalahar

Property is the fruit of labor-is a positive good in the world. That some should be rich, shows that others may become rich, and hence is just encouragement to industry and enterprise. Let not him who is homeless pull down the house of another, but let him work diligently and build one for himself, thus by example assuring that his own shall be safe from violence when built. -Abraham Lincoln,

The property which every man has in his own labor, as it is the original foundation of all other property, so it is the most sacred and inviolable. -Adam Smith

When action is divorced from consequences, no one is happy with the ultimate outcome. . . What private property does -- as the Pilgrims discovered -- is connect effort to reward, creating an incentive for people to produce far more. Then, if there's a free market, people will trade their surpluses to others for the things they lack. Mutual exchange for mutual benefit makes the community richer. -John Stossel

You shall not covet your neighbor's house, his field, his ox, his donkey, or anything that is your neighbors. -10th Commandment

Problems

The size of your problems is nothing compared with your ability to solve them. Don't overestimate your problems and underestimate yourself -Anonymous

Productivity

There are two technologies for producing automobiles in America. One is to manufacture them in Detroit, and the other is to grow them in Iowa. Everybody knows about the first technology; let me tell you about the second. First you plant seeds, which are the raw materials from which automobiles are constructed. You wait a few months until wheat appears. Then you harvest the wheat, load it into ships, and sail the ships westward into the Pacific Ocean. After a few months, the ships reappear with Toyotas on them. -Steven Landsburg

Work creates work. -Henry Hazlitt

The least productive people are usually the ones who are most in favor of holding meetings. -Thomas Sowell

Economies never lack consumption so long as there is production. -John Tamny

The triangle theory of production says you can only have two of these at the cost of the other: good, fast, and cheap. -Unknown

Windmills can't even produce enough energy to manufacture a windmill. -Ann Coulter

Get the plough, start planting now. –Norman Borlaug

When it is cheaper to make products through technology, there are more resources and people available to create new products that did not exist before thus increasing the standard of living, quality of life and life expectancy. -Dean Kalahar

It has been almost axiomatic, for at least a century, that the American economy produces more output than any other economy in the world. All this is so much taken for granted that no one considers it worth commenting on the fact that 300 million Americans today produce more output than more than a billion people in India or an even larger population in China — indeed, more than these two countries which, put together, have more than eight times the population of the United States. We also produce more than Japan, Germany, Britain, and France combined. -Thomas Sowell

The difference between carbon and diamonds is that diamonds stayed on the job longer. -Thomas Edison

Profiling

In New York...blacks constituted 78% of shooting suspects and 74% of all shooting victims in 2012, even though they are less than 23% of the city's population. Whites by contrast committed just over 2% of shooting victims and were under 3% of shooting victims in 2012, though they are 35% of the populace. Young black men in New York are 36 times more likely to be murdered than young white men- and their assailants are virtually always other black (or Hispanic) males... blacks at 55% of all police-stops subjects in 2012, are actually under-stopped compared with their 66% representation among violent criminals. –Heather Mac Donald

Profit/loss motive

It makes no sense to attack the risk taker when he is financially bankrupt, so intellectual consistency would guide us not to attack the risk taker when they are financially profitable. -Dean Kalahar

Profit is the cost of Capitalism; inefficiency is the cost of Socialism. -Thomas Sowell

While capitalism has a visible cost-profit-that does not exist under socialism, socialism has an invisible cost-inefficiency-that gets weeded out by losses and bankruptcy in capitalism. The fact that more goods are available more cheaply in a capitalist economy implies that profit is less costly than inefficiency. Put differently, profit is a price paid for efficiency. -Thomas Sowell

An economy robbed of failure is similarly one robbed of success. -John Tamny

Progressive

The term Progressive is a misnomer. It implies moving forward. But the so-called progressive movement is seeking not the expansion on individual freedom, liberty, and responsibility, but subservience of all to the ideology of centralized power in the hands of the elite. It is not moving forward, but moving in the opposite direction. It is a classic twisting of words to give them a palatable meaning to sell an unpalatable idea. Let's stop letting the left control our language and call them what they really are: Regressives. –Paul C. Ross

Psychology

To grow, you must change the recipe in life's cookbook. -Dean Kalahar

There is no heavier burden than having great potential.-Linus ('Peanuts')

Overbehaviors are an attempt for people to reduce self awareness.
-Dean Kalahar

Feeling good about oneself as a result of accomplishing a difficult task is far different than feeling full of yourself as the result of someone telling you how great you are. -Dean Kalahar

No one can make you feel inferior without your consent
-Eleanor Roosevelt

I have no money, no resources, no hopes. I am the happiest man alive.
-Henry Miller

If every instinct you have is wrong, then the opposite would have to be right. -Seinfeld

Jenny: Do you ever dream, Forrest, about who you're gonna be?
Forrest: Who I'm gonna be?
Jenny: Yeah.
Forrest: Aren't I going to be me? -Forrest Gump (movie)

In order to be whole you must first find what's missing. -Aly Bennett

It is never too late to be what you might have been. -George Eliot

It is much easier to deny and deconstruct facts than to come to terms with yourself. The taking of a personal inventory and accepting what nature and nurture has created brings with it a reality that many do not want to face. As a result, cognitive self survival tools are in play altering perception, behavior and moral judgments in lieu of dealing with unresolved personal issues or neurotic over-behaviors. -Dean Kalahar

If there are no moral absolutes then there is no need to deal with one's self because no judgments will be made. -Dean Kalahar

The road to self acceptance and understanding is far tougher than the route of outward expressions of inner turmoil. -Dean Kalahar

There is a little truth to everything they say. -Dean Kalahar

The nail that stands out gets pounded down. –Unknown

Gyroscopic people have internal guidance systems. Radar people steer according to signals bounced off others. -Davis Reisman

You might be able to fool them into believing you are who you say you are, but you can't fool yourself. -Jason Joseph

No longer wish "I could be," but accept the true me.–Madison Garriott

One of the symptoms of an approaching nervous breakdown is the belief that one's work is terribly important. -Bertrand Russell

"Hearing" what someone can't say can help you give him what he doesn't know he needs. –Kathy Brenneman

Tension is who you think you should be. Relaxation is who you are. -Chinese Proverb

It's the secrets that keep us sick. -Unknown

We don't stop playing because we grow old; we grow old because we stop playing. -George Bernard Shaw

Pain and suffering come from desire. -Buddah

Time heals almost everything. Give time time. -Regina Brett

Hearing what you want to hear is not listening. -Dean Kalahar

When they say "it's not about me", it really is about them - to them. -George Will

Fool me once, shame on you. Fool me twice, shame on me. -Chinese proverb

Half the harm that is done in this world is due to people who want to feel important. They don't mean to do harm-- but the harm does not interest them. Or they do not see it, or they justify it because they are absorbed in the endless struggle to think well of themselves." -T.S. Eliot

The more full of yourself your get, the less whole you become. -Dean Kalahar

There is no growth without risk, not only in economics but politics and daily living. -Jude Wanniski

Overbehaviors express on the outside the opposite of what's happening on the inside. -Dean Kalahar

Childhood lessons are not childish.-Dean Kalahar

Make peace with your past so it won't screw up the present.-Regina Brett

What you hate in another may be a reflection of what you hate in yourself. -Dean Kalahar

How is it you do not understand me when I speak? It is because you cannot bear to listen to my words. -John 8:43

People who are deeply invested in narcissism spend an awful lot of energy trying to maintain the illusion they have of themselves as being powerful and good, and they are exquisitely sensitive to anything that might prick that balloon. -William Anderson

Change is cathartic but routines are the condition of sanity. –Dean Kalahar

Nothing prevents us from being natural as much as the wish to look natural. -Francois de la Rochefoucauld

Overbehaviors are maladaptive coping strategies expressed in outward expressions of inner turmoil acting as a self-medicating attempt to heal a neurosis by exhibiting a pseudo opposite persona. -Dean Kalahar

Those who can't find self, destroy self. -Dean Kalahar

Not conforming is just conforming to the non-conformists. -Alex Krone

You are who you want to be. You are a fluid concept. You can stand out. Be self aware. Live in reality. Introspect. Go "cognitive." Don't be afraid of what others think. Learn. Explore. Experiment. Grow. Work towards self-actualization. Be happy with yourself. Love yourself. Appreciate your flaws. Go deeper. If there is something you don't like, change it. Use positive self talk. Listen to those who know you the best. Grow your self esteem, self concept, self worth, self respect self value, self awareness and self recognition. Decrease being self conscious. Life is too short to be unhappy and live in a way that isn't you. Don't define yourself by nouns. You can be your own person when all those "things" are gone. Change the recipe in life's cookbook. – Loving Pancakes, Black Crayons, and Other Things Mr. Kalahar has Taught Me. By Anna Brady

People persist in their self-destructive behavior, ignoring the blatant fact that what they've been doing for many years hasn't solved their problems? They think that they need to do it even more fervently or frequently, as if they were doing the right thing but simply had to try even harder.-Alan Deutschman

(he is) Like any man who destroys himself running for a finish line that doesn't exist –Wright Thompson

In order to go inward, you have to get "it" out. –Dean Kalahar

Don't underestimate the power of a sticker. –Dean Kalahar

The 64 box of Crayola's with the built in sharpener is a rite of passage. –Dean Kalahar

It's not called "them-worth" it's called self-worth. -Dean Kalahar

Losing is something you do, not something you are. –Elizabeth Spiegel

Serotonin, norepinephrine, and dopamine can be "tinkered with" by the psychopharmacologist yielding symptomatic relief and quantifiable benefit. However it is the wise clinician who looks beyond this view. People are so complex in the relationships we develop with ourselves, others, and our God, stress often results when any of these are strained, but relief comes when they are mended. *Often what is truly desired for healing is love*, which can come in many forms. Fortunately for our humanity, no medicine can take its place. –Kirt Micell, MD

The moment we decide to stop justifying every action is the moment our every action becomes justified. –Kayci Stone

A mind is an unfinished puzzle. Don't be afraid to try out new pieces. –Madison Olson

Before you *discover*, you must *uncover*. It is only then that you may *recover*. –Kent Thune

You have cognitive dissonance about being cognitively dissonant. –Former student

As long as you're green you're growing, as soon as you're ripe you start to rot. -Roy A. Kroc

"Life is like a mirror. Smile at it and it smiles back at you." -Peace Pilgrim

There is no better psychiatrist in the world than a dog licking your face. –Ben Williams

Race

In postmodern America, it is considered noble to prejudge people on the basis of their race and gender, but it can be ignoble to postjudge them on the basis of merit. –Victor Davis Hanson

Almost one half of the nation's murder victims that year were black and a majority of them were between the ages of 17 and 29. Black people accounted for 13% of the total U.S. population in 2005. Yet they were the victims of 49% of all the nation's murders. And 93% of black murder victims were killed by other black people, according to the same report...Less than half of black students graduate from high school...According to the U.S. Department of Education's Civil Rights Office, in the 2006-07 school year, 22% of all black and Hispanic K-12

111

students were suspended at least once (as compared to 5% of whites)…This year 22% of blacks live below the poverty line and a shocking 72% of black babies are born to unwed mothers. The national unemployment rate for black people increased last month to over 13%, nearly five points above the average for all Americans. –Juan Williams

The essence of contemporary blackness in America is eternal indignation. –John McWhorter

Everybody has asked the question ... 'What shall we do with the Negro?' I have had but one answer from the beginning. Do nothing with us! Your doing with us has already played the mischief with us. Do nothing with us! -Frederick Douglass

435 Americans are killed every 15 days in the U.S., the exact same number of people in Congress. The people killed and the killers are mostly black males… since 1980 over 600,000 people have been killed on the streets of America and that is "more than all the Americans killed in every war in the 20th Century." "If the Ku Klux Klan killed 200 black men in the city of Philadelphia, I can assure you that we would be on lockdown," said Nutter, "Every federal agency known to mankind would be up there trying to figure out what is going on. But 200 black men were killed in Philadelphia last year." –Walter Williams

What black America needs is not for white and other people to "understand" us or our past, but for us to be assisted in making our future brighter than our present, secure in "understanding" ourselves, thank you very much. -John McWhorter

Racism

As an observer on the national scene lo these many years, I have noted time and again that in a discussion of politics the first person to inject the topic of race into the discussion is often the racist.
–R. Emmett Tyrrell, Jr.

With segregation illegal and public racism considered a moral outrage, we black Americans are now told that we will not truly overcome until Americans don't even harbor private racist sentiment, until race plays not even a subtle role in America's social fabric. In other words, our current

battle is no longer against segregation or bigotry but "racism" of the kind that can be revealed only by psychological experiments and statistical studies. This battle is as futile as seeking a world without germs.
–John McWhorter

The term "institutional racism," which the Black Power movement injected into the lexicon in the late 1960s, is more damaging to the black psyche than the n-word or any crude jokes about plantations or food stamps. The term encourages blacks to think of society—in which inequality, while real, is complex and faceless—as actively and reprehensibly racist…The result is visceral bitterness toward something that can't feel or think. –John McWhorter

White liberals repeatedly state that America is a racist country, and that all whites are racist... But isn't that an admission that liberals are racist? When a person says, "We are all racists," isn't he saying that he is a racist?

A second proof that racism has a home on the left is the Left's primary argument against requiring all citizens to show identification when they vote. The liberal-left-Democratic argument is that such a requirement would greatly suppress the black vote. Thus, voter ID is racist…Will requiring ID really suppress the black vote?

The answer, shown in study after study, is no. Therefore, people who assume that voter ID would suppress the black vote have to believe that millions of blacks are uniquely incompetent citizens. Few things in civic life are simpler than obtaining an ID, and identification is needed almost everywhere in society. And is virtually every democracy in the world racist for requiring voter ID? Again, the answer is no. The idea is absurd.

So there are only two possibilities here. Either Democrats and the Left make this argument for political gain — to reinforce their hold on black voters by scaring them into believing that Republicans are racist — or the Left really believes that blacks are less competent than other groups are.

It is probable that both reasons — political opportunism and liberals' belief in black inferiority — are at work here. Most liberals, after all, do not believe that whites — even those who didn't graduate from high school — have any difficulty obtaining an ID, but they are certain that millions of blacks find this too onerous. This insult to black intelligence is as obvious as it is ignored.

Third is the liberal and left-wing advocacy for lowering standards for blacks — what is known as affirmative action. How is it not plain as daylight that whites (and other non-blacks) who argue for the continued lowering of standards for blacks have a low view of blacks? White liberals never advocate lowering professional or academic standards for, let us say, Asian immigrants who recently arrived in America, often without money or any knowledge of English. Why not? Because white liberals think that Asians are bright.

Finally, there is the Democratic and liberal opposition to school vouchers that would enable many black parents to send their children to schools superior to the awful ones that the (liberal-run) educational establishment has provided black children.

Most blacks want school vouchers, but most liberals vehemently oppose them. Why? Because what is good for teachers' unions is of more importance to the Left than what is good for blacks.

Who, then, is racist? By their own admission, and by the policies they pursue, the answer is the people who call themselves progressive.
–Dennis Prager

Radiation

The UN spent 25 years investigating the Chernobyl disaster and determined that 57 people died during the accident itself (including 28 emergency workers)…18 children died of thyroid cancer from drinking the milk from tainted cows…The most terrifying nuclear disaster in human history, which spread a cloud the size of 400 Hiroshima's across the whole of Europe killed 75 people…the 200,000 survivors of Hiroshima studied over 60 years found a 1% increase in cancer rates and no increase in inherited mutations.. The likelihood of work related death and injury for nuclear power plant workers is lower than for real estate agents…and stockbrokers. –Craig Nelson

Reality

Reality is fading away like the Cheshire cat, leaving behind only a smile that grows ever more alarming. -Henry Allen

Recycling

It's a waste of resources to preserve a material that is already abundant.
-Christina Daniel, Jessica Gordon, Matt Esola, Sagar Patel

Trees that newspapers are made from automatically recycled themselves for thousands of years before human being figured out how to plant seeds. -Thomas Sowell

It is more economical to throw out a product if the resources needed to replace it cost less than the resources necessary to fix it. -Dean Kalahar

Recycling is not categorically justified or unjustified, but is incrementally either worth or not worth the costs...-studies of government-imposed recycling programs in the United States have shown that what they salvage is usually worth less than the cost of salvaging it. -Thomas Sowell

The hallmark of science is a commitment to follow arguments to their logical conclusions; the hallmark of certain kinds of religion is a slick appeal to logic followed by a hasty retreat if it points in an unexpected direction.

Environmentalists can quote reams of statistics on the importance of trees and then jump to the conclusion that recycling paper is a good idea. But the opposite conclusion makes equal sense. I am sure that if we found a way to recycle beef, the population of cattle would go down, not up. If you want ranchers to keep a lot of cattle, you should eat a lot of beef. Recycling paper eliminates the incentive for paper companies to plant more trees and can cause forests to shrink. If you want large forests, your best strategy might be to use paper as wastefully as possible — or lobby for subsidies to the logging industry.

Mention this to an environmentalist. My own experience is that you will be met with some equivalent of the beatific smile of a door-to-door evangelist stumped by an unexpected challenge, but secure in his grasp of Divine Revelation.

This suggests that environmentalists — at least the ones I have met — have no real interest in maintaining the tree population. If they did, they would seriously inquire into the long-term effects of recycling. I suspect that they don't want to do that because their real concern is with the ritual of recycling itself, not with its consequences. The underlying

115

need to sacrifice, and to compel others to sacrifice, is a fundamentally religious impulse. –Steven Landsberg

By and large, it pays Americans to junk their cars, refrigerators, trolleys, and other capital equipment in a shorter time than it would pay people in poorer countries to do so. Nor is this a matter of being able to afford "waste." It would be a waste to keep repairing this equipment, when the same efforts elsewhere in the American economy would produce more than enough wealth to buy replacements.-Thomas Sowell

Relationships

I love you, and there is nothing you can do about it. -Lou Holtz

You should never give everything to someone, as you may end up as nothing in the end. -Erica Hostetler

Women are like apples on trees. The best ones are at the top. Most men don't want to reach for the good ones because they are afraid of falling & getting hurt. Instead they just take the rotten apples from the ground because it's easier. As a result, the apples at the top think something is wrong with them, when in reality, they're amazing. They just have to wait for the right man to come along, the one who's brave enough to climb all the way to the top of the tree. -Anonymous

I gave my all, but I think my all may have been too much.-Quincy Jones

We want what we can't have; we don't want what we have.
-Dean Kalahar

If we love someone that we formerly hated, that love will be greater than if hatred had not preceded it. -Benedict Spinosa

The best way to stay out of trouble is to breathe through your nose. That way you will keep your mouth shut. -Lou Holtz

Men lose more conquests by their own awkwardness than by any virtue in the woman. -Ninon de Lenclos

If you want a prince, act like a princess not a prostitute. If you want a queen, act like the king. -Dean Kalahar

If you're a no, let him know. -Dean Kalahar

They don't care how much you know. All they want to know is how much you care. –Unknown

Men fall in love with their eyes. Women fall in love with their ears. –Unknown

People are just waiting for an attractive person to do something they can interpret as liking them. -E.N. Aron

It's not the money that makes the man, it's the man that makes the money. -Dean Kalahar

Friendship is the cost of getting into a relationship. -Dean Kalahar

Taking "a break" is a prelude to the inevitable end. -Dean Kalahar

You are the music while the music lasts. -T.S. Eliot

You were always good enough for me; you were just never good enough for you. -She's Out of Her League (movie)

If you love him, let it be; he will find his way eventually. -Dean Kalahar

Men need to be needed, women need to be cherished. -John Grey

Modest is Hottest. -Ryan Peacock, Sarah Wilson

Talk without communication is just noise. -Dean Kalahar

Don't get married until your 29. -Dean Kalahar

Chemistry is not a substitute for physics. -Dean Kalahar

Love and sex are different. Don't confuse a feeling with a behavior.
-Dean Kalahar

"Overbehaviors" may make someone love you, but it's not you they really love. –Kelly Crocker

Men- you have the right to remain silent, anything you say can and will be used against you- by a woman. –Dean Kalahar

If it's easy, he thinks you're easy. –Dean Kalahar

Somehow the effort to stop clear-cut exploitation eventually morphed to include consensual sexual relationships where power was deemed "asymmetrical," so that even willing partners were seen as victims. Youth versus age was seen only in terms of administrative authority, not in terms of the erotic power of youthful beauty. In my time as a student and a professor, I saw four or five "asymmetrical" relationships in which much younger attractive graduate students made fools of aging nerdish professors, always to their own career advantage. The younger women in such relationships either dumped the power-brokers when the latter were no longer useful or filed complaints about being harassed if the dividends proved insufficient…In our bureaucratic and mechanistic society, we forget the Greeks' warning about the destructive and overarching power of youth, for which age and even a position of authority sometimes are no match. -Victor Davis Hanson

The power of a relationship lies on whoever cares less.
-The Ghost of Girlfriends Past. (movie)

It is better to suffer pain than to live in a world in which you don't allow yourself to be close enough to anybody to have the experience that's bound to give you suffering." And "love guarantees suffering."
-Eugene Kennedy via Peggy Noonan

We are never so defenseless against suffering as when we love.
-Sigmund Freud

How bold one gets when one is sure of being loved. –Sigmund Freud

Religion

We all have moral bank accounts, and it's good to make deposits because, God knows, we all make withdrawals. -Dennis Prager

People use the name of Jesus Christ every day. For many, it is employed as a curse. Few seek to silence those who blaspheme using His Name. Speak ill of the Prophet Muhammad and you risk a fatwa and crazies storming your house. Speak ill of Jesus Christ and no one will come to your door. He may be the last "religious" figure one can still crucify without penalty, at least in the short term. -Cal Thomas

Religion is not a hobby or a passing fancy, it is an instrumental part of what the founders saw as a necessary part to a civilization, To ignore this is to say you don't believe in civilization. -Stephen Carter

It is the duty of every man to render to the Creator such homage, and such only, as he believes to be acceptable to him. This duty is precedent both in order of time and degree of obligation, to the claims of Civil Society. Before any man can be considered as a member of Civil Society, he must be considered as a subject of the Governor of the Universe. -James Madison

Is it possible that God created natural selection and thus creationism and evolution are one and the same? -Dean Kalahar

Coincidence is God's way of remaining anonymous. -Albert Einstein.

If it's odd, it might be God. –Unknown

Every sinner has a future, every saint has a past. - Oscar Wilde

There are two kinds of people: those who say to God, "Thy will be done," and those to whom God says, "All right, then, have it your way -C.S. Lewis

Trust in the Lord with all your heart and lean not on your own understanding; in all your ways acknowledge him, and he will make your paths straight. -Proverbs 3:5-6

Sex and religion are closer to each other than either might prefer.
-Saint Thomas Moore

Real religion is the idea that if you believe, all may not go well, but, in the end, there is nothing to worry about. –James Martin

For your thoughts are not my thoughts, neither are your ways my ways.
–The Book of Isaiah

Faith offers not an explanation but the only reliable guide.
-Eugene Kennedy via Peggy Noonan

"Jesus humbled himself. He went from commanding angels to sleeping in the straw; from holding stars to clutching Mary's finger. The palm that held the Universe took the nail of a soldier. Why? Because that's what love does." –Max Lucado

Jesus is the only "man" in the history of the world to create a pure, unblemished, and monumental following of epic proportions. One might argue that is the tangible proof he is the son of God. –Dean Kalahar

If I have any belief about immortality, it is that certain dogs I have known will go to heaven- and very, very few persons. –James Thurber

All sin is a function of disordered desires- a distortion of love. The dammed either loved evil things or loved good things –in the wrong way…We can live when we dwell in love, at peace with God and our neighbors, our desires not denied but fulfilled in harmonious order.
–Rod Dreher

Saints aren't perfect, they're human. A saint is recognized for heroic virtue in the service of Christ, but saints have flaws, failings, and eccentricities. It is because they are not perfect that they are inspiring. They remind you what you could become. –Peggy Noonan

After he (Pope John Paul) was shot and almost killed in 1981, he made a point to go to the would-be assassin's prison cell to assure him that he was personally forgiven, and that God loved him. –Peggy Noonan

Republic

We are now forming a Republican form of government. Real Liberty is not found in the extremes of democracy, but in moderate governments. If we incline too much to democracy, we shall soon shoot into a monarchy, or some other form of dictatorship. -Alexander Hamilton

"Well, Doctor, what have we got—a Republic or a Monarchy?"
"A Republic, if you can keep it."-Benjamin Franklin

Rights

What's the difference between republican and democratic forms of government? John Adams captured the essence when he said, "You have rights antecedent to all earthly governments; rights that cannot be repealed or restrained by human laws; rights derived from the Great Legislator of the Universe." That means Congress does not grant us rights; their job is to protect our natural or God-given rights. -Walter Williams

The sacred rights of mankind are not to be rummaged for among old parchments or musty records. They are written as with a sunbeam, in the whole volume of human nature, by the hand of the divinity itself, and can never be obscured by mortal power. -Alexander Hamilton

The Constitution only gives people the right to pursue happiness. You have to catch it yourself. -Ben Franklin

You have rights antecedent to all earthly governments; rights that cannot be repealed or restrained by human laws; rights derived from the Great Legislator of the Universe. -John Adams

The right to swing my fist ends where the other man's nose begins. - Oliver Wendell Holmes

We throw the word "right" around wrong. –Dean Kalahar

Safety

Carrying "safety-first" to such extremes on all the millions of products in the economy would raise costs in general and correspondingly lower real income and living standard of the public. -Thomas Sowell

Sometimes safety precautions can be carried out to the point where they are fatal. -Thomas Sowell

Salesmen

"What happened to your face?" -sales pitch at a spa

Scarcity

Because of scarcity, we can only hope for a best case scenario between a myriad of choices, each having an associated cost. Wasting time with theoretical "what ifs" may make those with the time to fantasize about perfection smug, but it does little to raise the standard of living and quality of life for everyone. -Dean Kalahar

The first lesson of economics is scarcity; there is never enough of anything to satisfy all those who want it. The first lesson in politics is to disregard the first lesson of economics. -Thomas Sowell

Since the fiasco in the Garden of Eden, most of what we get is by sweat, strain, and anxiety. -Armen Albert Alchian

Second Amendment

Before a standing army can rule, the people must be disarmed; as they are in almost every kingdom of Europe. The supreme power in America cannot enforce unjust laws by the sword; because the whole body of the people are armed, and constitute a force superior to any band of regular troops that can be, on any pretence, raised in the United States.
-Noah Webster

No free man shall ever be debarred the use of arms. -Thomas Jefferson

The strongest reason for the people to retain the right to keep and bear arms is, as a last resort, to protect themselves against tyranny in government. -Thomas Jefferson

The Second Amendment is a doomsday provision . . . where all other rights have failed; where the government refuses to stand for reelection and silences those who protest; where courts have lost the courage to oppose, or can find no one to enforce their decrees . . . facing them unprepared is a mistake a free people get to make only once.
-Judge Alex Kozinski, 9th Federal Circuit Court of Appeals

This country was founded by religious nuts with guns. Who do (you) think stepped ashore on Plymouth Rock? -P.J. O'Rourke

Security

There is no security from existence itself. The only answer is to "plunge into" life. "We have to engage in life and take it on with all the risks it entails, or we won't be alive at all." -Eugene Kennedy via Peggy Noonan

Self interest

It is not from the benevolence of the butcher, the brewer, or the baker, that we expect our dinner, but from their regard to their own self-interest. -Adam Smith

How selfish however man may be supposed, there are evidently some principles in his nature which interest him in the fortune of others, and render their happiness necessary to him, though he derives nothing from it except the pleasure of seeing it. -Adam Smith

At some critical point, everyone makes choices based on incentives and his own perception of self-interest. -Victor Davis Hanson

When everyone has a distinct interest, men will not complain of one another, and they will make more progress, because everyone will be attending to his own business. - Aristotle

September 11, 2001

September 11, 2001, was chaos, sinister dust, mangled hunks of machinery, and primeval noises that sounded as if they came from the fiery, violent birth of the planet. That's what made the morning scary. It was the jumpers who gave the day its humanity. From the ground, it was impossible to imagine the hell going on inside those skyscrapers-turned-ovens. But when people appeared in the windows—91 stories high, with black smoke licking up into the air behind them—suddenly the enormity of the morning became clear. In the final seconds of life, by holding hands, a simple act of love, they denied evil. –Tim Townsend

Slavery

As I would not be a slave, so I would not be a master. –Abe Lincoln

Lincoln, the time is coming when we shall have to be all either Abolitionists or Democrats. –John Stuart

Socialism

Even though social engineers may feel well of themselves and their particular cause in lieu of dealing with personal insignificance, they do not have the right to place enormous costs on the lives of others.
-Dean Kalahar

One argument frequently heard is that the complexity of modern civilization creates new problems with which we cannot hope to deal effectively except by central planning. This argument is based on a complete misapprehension of the working of competition. The very complexity of modern conditions makes competition the only method by which a coordination of affairs can be adequately achieved…There would be no difficulty about efficient control or planning were conditions so simple that a single person or board could effectively survey all the facts. But as the factors which have to be taken into account become numerous and complex, no one center can keep track of them. The constantly changing conditions of demand and supply of different commodities can never be fully known, or quickly enough disseminated by any one center. -F.A. Hayek

That which is common to the greatest number has the least care bestowed upon it. –Aristotle

The champions of socialism call themselves progressives, but they recommend a system which is characterized by rigid observance of routine and by a resistance to every kind of improvement. They call themselves liberals, but they are intent upon abolishing liberty. They call themselves democrats, but they yearn for dictatorship. They call themselves revolutionaries, but they want to make the government omnipotent. They promise the blessings of the Garden of Eden, but they plan to transform the world into a gigantic post office. Every man but a subordinate clerk in a bureau. What an alluring utopia! What a noble cause to fight! Against all this frenzy of agitation there is but one weapon available: reason. Just common sense is needed to prevent man from falling prey to illusory fantasies and empty catchwords."
–Ludwig von Mises

Utopians will always be less happy than those who know that suffering is inherent to human existence. The utopian compares America to utopia and finds it terribly wanting. The conservative compares America to every other civilization that has ever existed and walks around wondering how he got so lucky as to be born or naturalized an American.
-Dennis Prager

Looking at what is promised under socialism, it is no wonder people are dazzled by what it offers. It is understandable that all humans would want these things. People might even believe they are possible. After all, if they can be envisioned, why can't they come to fruition? Sadly, however, utopian ideals are toppled by a world where humanity and scarcity come face to face. To ignore "what is" for the dream of "what could be" is a fatal miscalculation that has lead to disastrous results.
-Dean Kalahar

It is not soviet style communism that the American public is worried about. It is the worldview that is aligned with a command economy approach, notably socialism/progressivism, and the inevitable mutation into totalitarian government systems. "Soft" socialism is still socialism, and political elites that believe in a command approach are only a few steps away from the historically bad communists' like Stalin, Mao, Pol

Pot, Castro, Chavas, etc. The angst you see in America is about one specific natural law that is not negotiable- Freedom- and the attack against it by those whose world view is guided by the command approach to economics and politics. The public might not be able to articulate their instincts, but their instincts have told them to be aware - because when freedom is attacked, they know they are under attack.
-Dean Kalahar

The government under booth Herbert Hoover and Franklin Roosevelt, unlike under Coolidge, "chose to play God.
–Amity Shale via Benjamin Anderson

Social Justice

I never cease to be amazed at how often people throw around the lofty phrase "social justice" without the slightest effort to define it. It cannot be defined because it is an attitude masquerading as a principle.
-Thomas Sowell

Social justice" can easily become class warfare that polarizes a nation, while leading those at the bottom into the blind alley of resentments, no matter how many broad avenues of achievement may be available to them.–Thomas Sowell

In 1840, the theologian Luigi Taparelli d'Azeglio came up with the concept of social justice as a way to defend civil society from the ever-increasing intrusions of the state. Social justice, according to Taparelli, was the legitimate realm of justice beyond formal legal justice. Since then, the term has become completely inverted: "Social justice" has become an abracadabra phrase granting the state access to every nook and cranny of life. The only way for social justice to make sense is if you operate from the assumption that the invisible hand of the market should be amputated and replaced with the very visible hand of the state. In other words, each explicit demand for social justice carries with it the implicit but necessary requirement that the state do the fixing. And a society dedicated to the pursuit of perfect social justice must gradually move more and more decisions under the command of the state, until it is the sole moral agent. Social justice is a Trojan horse concealing a much more radical agenda. "Social justice" is a profoundly ideological term, masquerading as a generic term for goodness. In short, it is a tyrannical cliché. -Jonah Goldberg

For the civility police, the operational motto is always: "Do as we say, not as we do, in the name of social justice." –Michelle Malkin

Solutions

We fight fire with fire because the solution is often the problem.
–Dean Kalahar

Sophists

Today's sophists believe they can work within a vacuum outside the universal order while prudent pragmatists fear the explosion a vacuum unleashes upon its violation. -Dean Kalahar

Specialization

The woollen coat, for example, which covers the day labourer, as coarse and rough as it may appear, is the produce of the joint labour of a great multitude of workmen. The shepherd, the sorter of the wool, the wool-comber or carder, the dyer, the scribbler, the spinner, the weaver, the fuller, the dresser, with many others, must all join their different arts in order to complete even this homely production. How many merchants and carriers, besides, must have been employed in transporting the materials from some of those workmen to others who often live in a very distant part of the country! How much commerce and navigation in particular, how many ship-builders, sailors, sail-makers, rope-makers, must have been employed in order to bring together the different drugs made use of by the dyer, which often come from the remotest corners of the world! What a variety of labour too is necessary in order to produce the tools of the meanest of those workmen!... [I]f we examine, I say, all these things, and consider what a variety of labour is employed about each of them, we shall be sensible that without the assistance and cooperation of many thousands, the very meanest person in a civilized country could not be provided, even according to, what we very falsely imagine, the easy and simple manner in which he is commonly accommodated. - Adam Smith

Standards

Special thanks to the person who invented casual Friday. Now it's casual everyday in America. But when you lower standards people don't decide to give you more, they give you less.-Peggy Noonan

Straw man

(William F. Buckley describing Harvard economist John Kenneth Galbraith): a pyromaniac in a field of straw men.-George Will

Style

I think style just moved toward simplicity and eventually slipped into stupidity. -Linda Przybyszewski.

Sustainability

A Rolex might be the world's most sustainable product because it will always be repaired and passed down. –Jason Kibbey

Systemic causation (spontaneous order)

One of the core principles of the free market is that decisions are spread out among millions of people. These decisions, made out of self-interest, guide the economy and thus cause its evolution. -Dean Kalahar

Like a pebble thrown into a pond, choices are not self contained. The rippling effects are widespread and reach out to every corner. Determining the cause of economic change is like throwing a million pebbles into a raging river. -Dean Kalahar

Just as primitive peoples have tended to attribute such things as the swaying of trees in the wind to some intentional action by an invisible spirit, rather than to such systemic causes as variations in atmospheric pressure, so there is a tendency toward intentional explanations of systemic events in the economy, when people are unaware of the basic principles. -Thomas Sowell

Language is thus the epitome of an evolved complex order, with its own systemic characteristics, inner logic, and external social consequences-but without having been deliberately designed by any individual or council. Its rationality is systemic, not individual-an evolved pattern rather than an excogitated blueprint. -Thomas Sowell

The man of system, on the contrary, is apt to be very wise in his own conceit; and is often so enamoured with the supposed beauty of his own ideal plan of government, that he cannot suffer the smallest deviation from any part of it. He goes on to establish it completely and in all its parts, without any regard either to the great interests, or to the strong prejudices which may oppose it. He seems to imagine that he can arrange the different members of a great society with as much ease as the hand arranges the different pieces upon a chess-board. –Adam Smith

Taxation

Unchecked taxation for the purposes of income redistribution amounts to little more than government sponsored theft. -Walter Williams

Taxation may be so high as to defeat its object," so that sometimes, "a reduction of taxation will run a better chance, than an increase, of balancing the budget. -John Maynard Keynes

The subjects of every state ought to contribute towards the support of the government, as nearly as possible, in proportion to their respective abilities; that is, in proportion to the revenue which they respectively enjoy under the protection of the state. -Adam Smith

If 10 percent is good enough for the Baptist Church, it ought to be good enough for Congress. –Walter Williams

Taxation without representation is tyranny. -James Otis

In 1776 English taxes were in the range of 1 percent of income in most colonies, and possibly as high as 2.5 percent in the plantation colonies. For this, they went to war. –Gary North

Everyone wants to live at the expense of the state. They forget that the state wants to live at the expense of everyone. -Frederic Bastiat

The power to tax is the power to destroy. -John Marshall,

We have a system that increasingly taxes work and subsidizes non-work. -Milton Friedman

The tax balance that needs to be achieved is to give the state what it needs to protect you and your property while at the same time protecting you and your property from the state. -Dean Kalahar

We tax A to build B. The result is that we can see B but forget what A has and/or could have done. In short, we neglect to see the loss of what A could have produced. -Henry Hazlitt

Cutting government spending and government intrusion in the economy will almost surely involve immediate gain for the many, short-term pain for the few, and long-term gain for all. -Milton Friedman

The collection of taxes which are not absolutely required, which do not . . . contribute to the public welfare, is only a species of legalized larceny. -Calvin Coolidge

Taxing away what other people have earned, in order to finance one's own moral adventures, is often depicted as a humanitarian endeavor, while allowing others the same freedom and dignity as oneself, so they can make their own choices with their own earnings, is considered to be pandering to "greed." -Thomas Sowell

Government spending is taxation. –Milton Friedman

To compel a man to subsidize with his taxes the propagation of ideas which he disbelieves and abhors is sinful and tyrannical. -Thomas Jefferson

Governments create no wealth. They only move it around while taking a cut for their trouble. -John Stossel

A wise and frugal government, which shall restrain men from injuring one another, shall leave them otherwise free to regulate their own pursuits of industry and improvement, and shall not take from the mouths of labor the bread it has earned. -Thomas Jefferson

A government which lays taxes on the people not required by urgent public necessity and sound public policy is not a protector of liberty, but an instrument of tyranny. It condemns the citizen to servitude. –Calvin Coolidge

Outlays (taxes) all amount to plunder because they replace the invisible hand of the market with the hand of the state, and place political goals ahead of productive ones. -Amity Shlaes

Technology

When anyone can say anything, anyone will. When the guy in the basement having his third Grey Goose finally got a telephone line on AOL, he found out he could take his Id out for a ride. He could log on, indulge his angers, and because it was anonymous he never had to stand behind his words or defend them, He never had to be embarrassed in front of his kids. The internet is a breakthrough in human freedom. But over the last 20 years it has had a certain leveling effect. It hypes the cheap and glitzy, it reduces the worthiness of a thought to the number of clicks it gets. -Peggy Noonan

Smart machines are simply the pumps that deliver the water of knowledge — not knowledge itself. –Victor Davis Hanson

What does it matter that millions of American students can communicate across thousands of miles instantly with their iPads and iPhones if a poorly educated generation increasingly has little to say? –Victor Davis Hanson

The latest fad of near-insolvent universities is to offer free iPads to students so that they can access information more easily. But what if most undergraduates still have not been taught to read well or think inductively, or to have some notion of history? Speeding up their ignorance is not the same as imparting wisdom. Requiring a freshman Latin course would be a far cheaper and wiser investment in mastering

131

language, composition, and inductive reasoning than handing out free electronics. –Victor Davis Hanson

Tolerance

In the 1960s, radical philosopher Herbert Marcuse popularized the "repressive tolerance" theory of modern progressives."Liberating tolerance would mean intolerance against movements from the right and toleration of movements from the left," Marcuse pontificated. "Certain things cannot be said, certain ideas cannot be expressed, certain policies cannot be proposed." –Michelle Malkin

Trade

The most important single central fact about a free market is that no exchange takes place unless both parties benefit. -Adam Smith

Imports do not represent failure. -Matt Slaughter

Gold has no nationality. -Charles de Gaulle

Don't shoot a hole in your side of the boat just because the other man in the boat shot a hole on his side. -Walter Williams

Exports and imports are flip sides of the same coin. Exports are necessary to generate the earnings to pay for imports, or exports are the goods a country must give up in order to acquire imports. Exports and imports are inherently interdependent, and any policy that reduces one will also reduce the other. -Douglas A. Irwin.

When goods can't cross borders freely, armies inevitably do.
-Cordell Hull

Tariffs always scare investors because they ensure economic inefficiency through the subsidization of the weak at the expense of the strong.
-John Tamny

Tribalism

The story of modernity is the story of how we moved away from traditional, non-voluntary forms of tribalism based on familial, ethnic, or even nationalistic lines and toward voluntary forms of tribalism (individual liberty). The American founding was revolutionary in its embrace of the universality of human rights (even as it fell so short of its own ideals with the institution of slavery). Since then, the West has fought several civil wars to break away from various tribal ideologies, including not just monarchism and imperialism but also Nazism (racial tribalism), Communism (economic tribalism), and fascism (national tribalism). –Jonah Goldberg

Tyranny

The welfare of humanity is always the alibi of tyrants. -Albert Camus

Resistance to tyrants is obedience to God.-Thomas Jefferson

These are the times that try men's souls. The summer soldier and the sunshine patriot will, in this crisis, shrink from the service of their country; but he that stands by it now, deserves the love and thanks of man and woman. Tyranny, like hell, is not easily conquered; yet we have this consolation with us, that the harder the conflict, the more glorious the triumph. -Thomas Paine

Of all tyrannies, a tyranny exercised for the good of its victims may be the most oppressive. It may be better to live under robber barons than under omnipotent moral busybodies. The robber baron's cruelty may sometimes sleep, his cupidity may at some point be satiated; but those who torment us for our own good will torment us without end, for they do so with the approval of their own conscience. - C.S. Lewis

Unemployment

It is far better to suffer unemployment at the hands of a free state than to suffer through the dictates of totalitarian fate. -Dean Kalahar

Unforeseen consequences

Man may be able to fly to the moon, build homes on the beach, or clone sheep, but that does not mean space ships will not blow up, homes will not be lost to hurricanes and cloning sheep will not lead to unforeseen consequences. -Dean Kalahar

Once you open the floodgates, you can't tell the water where to go. -Thomas Sowell

Unions

No entity is ensured perpetual union. The process of forming nations and empires and then disassembling them back into small city states or provincial units is certainly not novel, but rather ancient, and more likely fluid and cyclical than linear — even if the process takes decades or at times centuries. When an empire or even a nation state can no longer guarantee locals that the increased security and wealth of a vast union makes it well worth transcending their parochial customs and ethnic profiles, then we have a Greece of 1,500 city states, or a medieval Europe of castles and moats. -Victor Davis Hanson

Visions/worldviews

The vision of human limits offers a best case view, while the vision of ever expanding human capacity pushes civilization in a direction that will ultimately create a scenario of human decline. -Friedrich A. Hayek

The humanistic vision blindly believes man can alter forces more powerful than they can comprehend. The ability for man to reason without limits is in of itself its fatal error in reasoning and thus its downfall. -Friedrich A. Hayek

In the early 19th century a liberal was a person who favored personal and economic liberty; that is freedom from the control and power of the state. A conservative was originally a person who opposed the excesses of the French Revolution and its emphasis on personal freedom and favored a restoration of the power of the state, the church and the aristocracy. -James Q. Wilson

Any 20 year-old who isn't a liberal doesn't have a heart, and any 40 year-old who isn't a conservative doesn't have a brain. -Winston Churchill

To the universal/natural/conservative/classical liberal mind passion without principle is just emotion; to the humanistic/synthetic/liberal/classical conservative mind, emotion is misread as principled thought. -Dean Kalahar

For the classical liberal/modern conservative: Faith is placed in God upon a humbled acceptance of the limits to man's reason because of a flawed human nature. "If it can't be reasoned, that does not mean it does not exist." For the classical conservative/modern liberal: Faith is placed in reason and the unlimited potential of an infallible ego-centric man. "If it can't be reasoned, it does not exist."-Dean Kalahar

Christians aren't people who believe they are without sin; they're people who know they're sinners and are awestruck by God's grace in sending his only Son to take the punishment they deserve. This is in contradistinction to liberals, all of whom believe they're on a fast track to heaven on the basis of being "basically good" people -- and also believe that anyone who disagrees with that theological view is evil. -Ann Coulter

The Right is preoccupied with fighting evil and the Left is preoccupied with fighting those who fight evil. –Dennis Prager

Vivid exception/ anecdote

The vivid exception does not trump reason. -Dean Kalahar

Just as when the wind blows a leaf upward, the law of gravity remains intact. –James Dorn

Anecdote, the age-old enemy of logic, now reigns supreme and trumps induction — as if the exception is always proof of the rule, as if the public will always forsake reason for emotion. Forget the statistics on Obamacare — my Uncle Joe was denied coverage after he lost his job. The economy is getting better, because my friend Will was offered a job today. Why enforce federal immigration law, when there is no nicer window washer than Herlinda, who comes to my house every Tuesday? It hailed in June here; therefore the world must be experiencing climate change. I would never shoot an AR-15, and therefore there is no need for anyone else to. My nephew is gay, and he's a great guy; therefore gay marriage is great too. Sally yesterday lifted heavier weights than did three guys in the gym: Presto, female soldiers can do anything that male soldiers can. -Victor Davis Hanson

Wages

One may have the same job but not do the same job.-Dean Kalahar

Wages should be left to the fair and free competition of the market, and should never be controlled by the interference of the legislature.
-David Ricardo

If the worker can't compete, they can either change and become more productive or support a union that will protect their inefficiencies.
-Dean Kalahar

To say that a shoe shine boy earns "too little" or a surgeon "too much" is to say that third parties should have the right to preempt the decisions of those who elected to spend their money on shoes or surgery.
-Thomas Sowell

War

War is evil but it is not the only evil. -Unknown

The great curse of the 20th century was the inability of decent people to realize that what was unthinkable to them was both thinkable and doable by others- like Hitler, Stalin, Mao and Pol Pot. -Thomas Sowell

From 1917 to its collapse in 1991, the Soviet Union murdered about 62 million of its own people. During Mao Zedong's reign, 35,236,000, possibly more, Chinese citizens were murdered. All together 76 million Chinese were killed by Zedong and his successors. By comparison, Hitler's Nazis managed to murder 21 million of its citizens and citizens in nations they conquered. Adding these numbers to the 60 million lives lost in war makes the 20th century mankind's most brutal era. -Walter Williams & Rudolph J. Rummel

In this era of non-judgmental mush, too many Americans have become incapable of facing the brutal reality of unprovoked hatred based on envy, resentment and ultimately on a vicious urge to lash out against others for the pain of one's own insignificance. -Thomas Sowell

As a society, we shouldn't seek moral equivalency, because we are then doomed to live according to the lowest standards of humanity. But we also don't live in a moral vacuum. We don't live in a utopia. We're in a war...To suggest we violated cultural norms in a way that the people of the region don't do is to give the people of the region a pass. The legacy of the degradation of bodies in the Afghanistan-Pakistan region is historical. −Asra Nomani

The Bible tells us there is a time for all things, and there is a time to preach and a time to pray. But the time for me to preach has passed away; and there is a time to fight and that time has now come. -Rev Peter Gabriel Muhlenberg

The causes of war as discerned ever since Thucydides' time are three: wars of ideology, of fear, and of gain. -Charles Hill

To the ancient Greek philosophers Heraclitus and Plato, war was the father of us all, while peace was a brief parenthesis in the human experience. -Victor Davis Hanson

War involves people killing one another and the destruction of wealth, while economic growth is a function of people working with one another on the war to creating wealth. War is by its very name anti-economic growth precisely because it's about destruction of the human, financial and physical capital that drives economic growth, yet those who claim to be "economists" laughably, and rather horrifyingly, suggest that war represents stimulus. −John Tamny

Wealth

In a free society, wealth is not distributed - it is earned. -Walter Williams

137

The way to make the most money in a capitalistic economy is to offer a better "mousetrap" at a lower cost, to as many people as possible.
-Dean Kalahar

We might think of dollars as being 'certificates of performance.' The better I serve my fellow man and the higher the value he places on that service, the more certificates of performance he gives me. The more certificates I earn, the greater my claim on the goods my fellow man produces. That's the morality of the market. In order for one to have a claim on what his fellow man produces, he must first serve him.
-Walter Williams

Serving one's fellow man to acquire wealth also has a tempering effect on the abusive behaviors associated with greed for power, because it is difficult to exploit others when you are forced to serve them.
-Dean Kalahar

The rich adopt novelties and become accustomed to their use. This sets a fashion which others imitate. Once the richer classes have adopted a certain way of living, producers have an incentive to improve the methods of manufacture so that soon it is possible for the poorer classes to follow suit. This luxury furthers progress. Innovation is the whim of an elite before it becomes a need of the public. The luxury today is the necessity of tomorrow. Luxury is the road maker of progress: it develops latent needs and makes people discontented. In so far as they think consistently, moralists who condemn luxury must recommend the comparatively desireless existence of the wild life roaming in the woods as the ultimate ideal of civilized life. -Ludwig Von Mises

Not understanding the process of a spontaneously-ordered economy goes hand in hand with not understanding the creation of resources and wealth. And when a person does not understand the creation of resources and wealth, the only intellectual alternative is to believe that increasing wealth must be at the cost of someone else. This belief that our good fortune must be an exploitation of others may be the taproot of false prophecy about doom that our evil ways must bring upon us.
-Julian Simon

Spending money you don't have to make you look rich is poor.
—Dean Kalahar

Capital is wealth in the form of private ownership of valued resources in which surplus value is added and then traded voluntarily in the market to meet real demands. That's why "money never fed a hungry child."
–Dean Kalahar

There are many competing definitions of "rich," and they usually involve a percentage: the top 10 percent, the top 5 percent, the dreaded 1 percent. My own definition is the point at which the marginal utility of an additional dollar for personal consumption and investment is effectively zero... The Fitzgeraldian rich — "different from you and me" — are indeed a class apart, though the history of modern capitalism is one of making membership in that rarefied grouping much more democratic than it ever has been. What was within living memory a class in the true sense of that word — aristocrats and heirs and the odd movie star — is today an aggregate that contains relatively few people whose economic talents consist of choosing their parents wisely and a great many more formerly middle-class manufacturers of plumbing fixtures.
-Kevin Williamson

Data from the Bureau of Labor Statistics finds that among the allegedly privileged 1 percent, inherited wealth accounts for only 15 percent of household holdings, a smaller share than it does among middle-class families.- Kevin Williamson

Many self-styled progressives today are willing to sacrifice the standard of living of billions of poor people, in order to prevent a few people from becoming really rich. –Robert Murphy

No one is poorer because Bill Gates, Larry Ellison, et al., are so much richer. –John Steele Gordon

Welfare

The democracy will cease to exist when you take away from those who are willing to work and give to those who would not. -Thomas Jefferson

I predict future happiness for Americans if they can prevent the government from wasting the labors of the people under the pretense of taking care of them. -Thomas Jefferson

Because there is no clear line between sickness and health, and where you stand on the continuum is bound up with individual choice, the more medical services are provided by the State as a part of welfare, the more the programs reinforce the conditions that bring about the need to make use of them. -Frederick Hayek

Nobody but a beggar chuses to depend chiefly upon the benevolence of his fellow citizens. -Adam Smith

Have you ever been to Yosemite or the Grand Canyon or anyplace that's a national park? Well, if you go, let me tell you what you'll encounter. You'll encounter signs everywhere telling you not to feed the animals. And the reason that you are not to feed the animals ... the animals must learn to fend for themselves if they are to survive and thrive. When you feed animals they become dependent and no longer function as nature intends... "A fed animal is a dead animal," is one such sign. So the very government, the very bureaucracy that wants you kept on welfare, The same people, who if you go to a state park will not let you feed the animals because they will become dependent, just like you were. And they won't be able to survive, just like you couldn't. And they won't be able to fend for themselves, just like you couldn't. And they won't be able to feed themselves, and they won't be able to thrive, and they will not be able to detect danger and so forth. So they know, but they want you to stay dependent. They want you to stay on welfare.
-Rush Limbaugh

The government does not support the people, the people support the government. -Robert Ingersoll

Big Government ...is a girl's best friend, the sugar daddy whose checks never bounce. -Mark Stein

Dependency is a problem for rich and poor alike. –John Tamny

The labors of thirty or forty honest and industrious men shall not be consumed to maintain a hundred and fifty idle loiterers.
-John Smith at Jamestown in 1609

When you pay people for being low income, you are going to have more low income people. - Casey Mulligan

If taxing (costing) smokers gets you less smokers; then paying people to not work- gets you less workers. -Dean Kalahar via Casey Mulligan

White Privilege

There is a phrase that floats around college campuses, that threatens to strike down opinions without regard for their merits, but rather solely on the basis of the person that voiced them. "Check your privilege," ... a reminder that I ought to feel personally apologetic because white males seem to pull most of the strings in the world.

I do not accuse those who "check" me and my perspective of overt racism, although the phrase, which assumes that simply because I belong to a certain ethnic group I should be judged collectively with it, toes that line. But I do condemn them ...for ascribing all the fruit I reap not to the seeds I sow but to some invisible patron saint of white maleness who places it out for me before I even arrive.

That's the problem with calling someone out for the "privilege" which you assume has defined their narrative. You don't know what their struggles have been, what they may have gone through to be where they are. Assuming they've benefitted from "power systems" or other conspiratorial imaginary institutions denies them credit for all they've done, things of which you may not even conceive.

The truth is, though, that I have been exceptionally privileged in my life, albeit not in the way any detractors would have it...
Behind every success, large or small, there is a story, and it isn't always told by sex or skin color. My appearance certainly doesn't tell the whole story, and to assume that it does and that I should apologize for it is insulting. While I haven't done everything for myself up to this point in my life, someone sacrificed themselves so that I can lead a better life. But that is a legacy I am proud of. I have checked my privilege. And I apologize for nothing. - Tal Fortgang

Wisdom

We shall not grow wiser before we learn that much that we have done was very foolish. -F.A. Hayek

Wisdom begins with reverence for God. –Biblical

Writing

All faults in comprehension are the responsibility of the writer. –William Safire

Made in the USA
Columbia, SC
21 November 2024

47209468R00078